Better Homes and Gardens®

LIVING
· THE ·
COUNTRY LIFE

College of the Ouachitas

BETTER HOMES AND GARDENS® BOOKS
Editor: Gerald M. Knox
Art Director: Ernest Shelton
Managing Editor: David A. Kirchner

Furnishings and Design Editor: Shirley Van Zante
Senior Furnishings Editor: Pamela Wilson Cullison

Associate Art Directors: Linda Ford Vermie, Neoma Alt West, Randall Yontz
Copy and Production Editors: Marsha Jahns, Mary Helen Schiltz, Carl Voss,
    David Walsh
Assistant Art Directors: Harijs Priekulis, Tom Wegner
Senior Graphic Designers: Alisann Dixon, Lynda Haupert, Lynn Neymeyer
Graphic Designers: Mike Burns, Mike Eagleton, Deb Miner, Stan Sams,
    D. Greg Thompson, Darla Whipple

Vice President, Editorial Director: Doris Eby
Executive Director, Editorial Services: Duane L. Gregg

General Manager: Fred Stines
Director of Publishing: Robert B. Nelson
Vice President, Retail Marketing: Jamie Martin
Vice President, Direct Marketing: Arthur Heydendael

Living the Country Life
Editor: Pamela Wilson Cullison
Copy and Production Editor: Marsha Jahns
Graphic Designer: Tom Wegner
Electronic Text Processor: Donna Russell

Contents

Introduction

It is little wonder that country has such widespread appeal. In addition to being a wonderfully warm and easily adaptable decorating style, country is—for many people—a way of life as well. And because the look can be interpreted in myriad ways, city dwellers and suburbanites are just as likely as rural residents to incorporate country into their homes. The big and beautiful Better Homes and Gardens® *Living the Country Life* book covers country from all these points of view, both inside and outside the house.

Country: A State Of Mind

Say the word "country" to ten different people and it's likely to evoke ten different visions. Unlike any other decorating style, country is not just a look, but often a way of life as well. This isn't to say that devotees of country don't share a common denominator. The one thread that connects them all—to the look and the life-style—is a shared appreciation for the simple, unpretentious objects and attitudes of the past.

Like a long, winding road, the country life-style meanders in many directions—from a rural landscape to the suburbs and the city. Whatever the setting, country style appeals to those who seek harmony with nature and take pleasure in the simple things of life. Going on picnics and walks through the woods; attending auctions, crafts festivals, and fairs; watching the sunrise; finding fascination in folk art and handcrafted things; working in the garden; making quilts and weaving; or just sitting by the fireside with friends—these are just a few of the lures of living the country life.

Country as a decorating
style cannot be
pigeonholed into a single,
static look. For every person
who is captivated by the
hand-hewn and the
homespun of early
Americana, there are others
who are equally enthralled
with the time-honored
offerings of England and
other faraway places. Each
kind of country has its own
personality and decorative
appeal. Whether you're
attracted to the rustic or the
refined, to old-fashioned
comfort or uptown style,
country acclimates easily
and beautifully to any
environment.

Country
Close-Ups

A Cozy Cape Cod Cottage

Seen through the sheltering branches of a mulberry tree planted more than 200 years ago, this 1777 Cape Cod house was built by a Massachusetts sea captain. Now lovingly and carefully renovated inside and out, the dwelling is a year-round country retreat for owners Marjorie and Donald Penny.

It took the Pennys 10 years to find the house of their dreams, and several more to structurally and decoratively revive the sadly run-down structure. Friends and relatives saw the house as an irredeemable has-been, but Marjorie—an interior designer—saw, in her mind's eye, an enchanting cottage just waiting to emerge. And beautifully emerge it did, as you will see on the following 10 pages.

continued

15

A Cozy
Cape Cod Cottage
(continued)

L ow ceilings in the Pennys'
living room naturally evoke
a cozy cottage look. The snug
feeling is further enhanced by
the large-scale floral print wall
covering and the companion
fabric used for the simple swag-
and-jabot window treatment.
The same summery fabric
shows up again on the comfy
armchair in the foreground.

Other furnishings include a
down-filled sofa trimmed in a
rose-color fringe, two armless
slipper chairs covered in dark
green and pink floral chintz,
and an antique tea table, appro-
priately set for afternoon tea.
(The view *above* shows the same
table in its "everyday" mien.)
On the wall behind the sofa
is a framed 18th-century sheep
painting and, above it, an old
"courting" mirror, so-called
because a comb and brush set
hang inside it. *continued*

17

A Cozy
Cape Cod Cottage
(continued)

Designed for the pursuit of peace and quiet, the library is a comfortable, shut-out-the-world retreat. This is where the Pennys gravitate at the end of a busy workweek to read, listen to music, or just relax by the warmth of the fire. In contrast to the light, airy ambience of the living room, the library is deliberately dark and snug. The woodwork is painted high-gloss deep amethyst, and the walls are papered in a small, cream-color fleur-de-lis pattern on the same amethyst background.

Adding to the room's sense of repose are meant-for-relaxing furnishings. Marjorie's favorite spot is the rolled-arm chair and

ottoman in front of the fire-place. Don prefers to put his feet up, literally and figurative-ly, on the old one-arm Victorian sofa, *above.* Both Pennys take great pleasure in reading, and three walls of floor-to-ceiling built-in bookshelves handsome-ly attest to the fact.

Country accessories are few but effective. Providing a flight of fancy at the fireplace wall is a hand-carved weathered wood crane. The ceramic lamb stand-ing in front of the window, *above,* was found at a butcher shop in England. The elaborate necklace dangling from the lamb's neck is the kind worn by real lambs in Greece.

A Cozy
Cape Cod Cottage
(continued)

The rear of the Penny house features a new 30x30-foot brick terrace that often is used for *alfresco* entertaining. To facilitate the comings and goings of guests, the new kitchen wing incorporates two sets of French doors that open to the terrace from both the dining and cooking ends of the kitchen.

To contrast with the brick and to cool off this south-facing sun pocket, the new exterior shingles were left to weather to a silvery gray. The rest of the exterior is painted mulberry red, in honor of the venerable tree at the front of the house.

Above, a cobblestone path at the side of the house is bordered by a lovely aromatic herb garden and newly built white picket fence.   *continued*

A Cozy
Cape Cod Cottage
(continued)

Marjorie Penny is a master at melding the past with the present. Rather than limit her newly remodeled kitchen/dining area to a single design scheme, she culled from various style sources, old and new.

The kitchen work area is mostly modern in feeling. Cupboards are white-painted pine, embellished with clear crystal knobs. Counters are pastel yellow laminate, and the floor is surfaced with Mexican tiles laid on the diagonal.

Providing a beautiful transition between the kitchen and dining area is an old scrubbed pine chest from England. It serves not only as a room divider, but provides extra counter space and storage as well.

Pictured *above* is an old cupboard depicting fanciful hand-painted country scenes. *continued*

Every room of the Penny house is steeped in style and character. The master bedroom is particularly charming, with its flowered walls and draperies and its high-gloss white painted floor. The four-poster is a 20-year-old reproduction that's been treated to a new chintz canopy, skirt, and coverlet. The small, graceful storage armoire dates from the mid-1800s; the painted desk and chair are new.

Even the upstairs hallway, *above*, is replete with personality. The painted floor and stair treatment—a creation of Marjorie's—consists of a white base coat spattered (by hand and by brush) with pink, amethyst, and seafoam green paint. Two coats of clear polyurethane protect the finished effect.

Home for An Avid Collector

For Pat and David Payne, of Marblehead, Massachusetts, living the country life is both a personal and professional pleasure. As a couple, the Paynes share an interest in restoring and refurbishing old houses. On an individual basis, Pat, an interior designer, owns a firm that specializes in country antiques and accessories.

The Paynes' most recent renovation project is the 1716 sailmaker's house pictured here. Known at one time as "Spite House" (a name acquired when several families owned parts of the house and refused to sell to each other), the dwelling today is filled, not with spite, but with a fascinating collection of folk art and country antiques.

Pat's personal collection ranges from rocking horses in every size and shape, to carrousel figures, antique carriages, old cradles, and antique toys. In the living room, *left*, a sampling of Pat's collection keeps company with sink-down comfortable seating. *continued*

Home for an
Avid Collector
(continued)

I t took a major face-lift, both inside and out, to restore the gone-to-seed structure. Walls, ceilings, and floors—all were in terrible condition. But the Paynes, being fervent old-house buffs, were intrigued, not intimidated, by the challenge.

Important remodeling changes in the dining room included removing the plaster ceiling to create a rustic look. Exposed beams and rafters were sand-blasted, and freestanding pipes from a bathroom above were relocated. Wide-plank pine floorboards, like those in the living room, replaced a nothing-special narrow-board oak floor. To brighten the room, a solid wall was removed to accommo-date a large multipane window.

Venerable furnishings include an old farm table accompanied by six bow-back Windsor chairs, an antique pine dry sink (now used for linen storage), and a colorful Oriental rug. The graceful wire-arm chandelier is a new reproduction. Here again, Pat's penchant for old rocking horses is evident. *continued*

The Paynes' country kitchen/ family room is all new, though many old materials were cleverly recycled in the redo. The old room was gutted, new windows were added to admit more light, and a used-brick fireplace was introduced where previously there had been none. An old barn beam serves as a rugged fireplace mantel. Additional barn beams and old attic boards were used to create a new, but old-looking, ceiling.

The cozy seating area has the look of built-in banquettes, but, in fact, is composed of contemporary sectional seating covered in easy-care chocolate brown vinyl. Big pillows in colorful country French prints beckon passersby to sit in comfort. The glass lampshade is an unsigned Tiffany design.

Standing guard in front of the fireplace is a beguiling bear from a European carrousel. At one time, Pat had many such carrousel figures, but because they take up so much room, she has pared her collection to a favorite few. *continued*

Home for an Avid Collector

(continued)

In a deliberate departure from the rustic attitude of the rest of the house, the Paynes' new master bedroom retreat, though still country in spirit, has uncluttered contemporary leanings.

In creating the room, the Paynes relied on Ted Haggett, a master craftsman used to working with old houses, and a genius at making new wood look old. Haggett changed the total configuration of the space by removing the ceiling and exposing the room to its peak. New beams were added for support and appearance.

This is the only room in the house with wall-to-wall carpet. Pat chose wool in a pale, natural tone for its tranquil, room-warming qualities.

The king-size brass-and-iron bed was ordered from a catalog and given a European look with a big feather pouf covered in a French provincial cotton print. Both the pouf and the bed skirt are bordered and ruffled, as are the pillows and bolsters.

Tiered window shutters, stained to match the woodwork, are in keeping with the room's simplified country character.

The old cradle to the right of the rocking horse is used as a repository for extra pillows, quilts, and old toys.

New Looks For an Old Farmhouse

Time, far from taking its toll on this 1847 farmhouse, has been beautifully beneficial. Outside, nature deserves most of the credit. Years of weathering by wind and rain have turned the shingled siding to its present shade of silvery gray. Time, too, is responsible for turning a small sapling into the magnificent American elm that now shelters the house in leafy, sun-dappled splendor.

The lovely summer porch, *above*, with its ceiling painted to simulate the sky, is an idyllic adjunct to the dwelling. *continued*

New Looks for
An Old Farmhouse
(continued)

Thanks to the efforts of designer Claudia Sargent, the interior of the farmhouse has taken a beautiful leap toward the 20th century. In the living room, a combination of country and contemporary influences adds up to a crisp, non-cliché look that's comfortable and easy to maintain.

Though the plump, modular seating pieces are modern-day casual, they're covered in a country-inspired windowpane check. The pillow fabrics represent provincial designs from France, Finland, and India. The coffee table looks contemporary because of its simple lines, but is actually made of old planks from a leather tanning factory that was once the homeowner's family business.

The painted cupboard in the corner is a circa-1800 heirloom from Bavaria. Used for storing accessories, the piece is a beautiful example of Westphalian peasant art. The old copper pieces on top of the cupboard are German.

Newly installed sliding glass doors are other pleasing additions from modern times. One door leads to the porch; the other to a new redwood deck that hugs the rear exterior. Both doors offer splendid views of the enchanting meadowland that surrounds the house.

continued

New Looks for
An Old Farmhouse
(continued)

S haker-like in its simplicity, the dining room is a good example of country decorating without furbelows.

Because this is a room for a family with three grown daughters who often bring friends to dinner, a large table was a must. Like the coffee table in the living room, the dining table has sentimental as well as practical value. (It, too, was made from the wood that lined the old leather tanning vats in the family business.) In slick contrast to the wood, the twin table bases are high-tech red-lacquered pedestals from a restaurant supply firm. For more contrast, the new rush-seat ladder-back chairs are pale natural ash, cushioned with tie-on pads covered in Indian cotton. Bare wide floorboards are pine, lightened to match the tone of the table.

Contributing to the room's unstudied charm is the vignette grouping of child-size bentwood furniture—all original Thonet pieces that came from the homeowner's late husband's nursery.

The sideboard is a European dough trough that dates to the early 1800s. Accessories on and around this lovely antique include an old Guatemalan horse with rider, brass candlesticks, a ceramic bowl, and a delightful Haitian folk art painting.

The simple window treatment consists of unlined cotton curtains in a grid pattern of navy on white.   *continued*

New Looks for
An Old Farmhouse
(continued)

The second story of this wonderful old farmhouse is just as inviting as the first. The master bedroom is particularly delightful, with its bright and breezy personality inspired by the yellow-painted floor.

The secret to achieving such a slick and shiny surface is to first sand the wood until it is absolutely smooth and free of flaws, dust, and grit. The next step is to apply at least two coats of deck enamel, letting the first coat dry completely before applying the second. Once the enamel has dried, two coats of high-gloss polyurethane are added to seal and protect the painted finish.

In accompaniment with the colorful floor is a simple mix of furnishings. Two early Hitchcock chairs, an old writing desk, and an informal wicker chair are staged like sculpture against stark white walls. The queen-size bed is situated to take in the view of the great outdoors. The roof deck just beyond the open door is a favorite spot for bird-watching, reading, and basking in the sun.

A House With Formal Flair

When Mary Ann and Bob Kovac come home to their suburban colonial dwelling, there's little to remind them that they're just a few miles from downtown St. Louis. Ringed by trees, gardens, and a pond stocked with fish, their home is a haven from life's hustle and bustle, country in attitude if not in fact.

Though Bob must commute to the city each day, Mary Ann gets to stay put. Her country antiques shop, "Unicorn Collections, Ltd.," is located just a few steps from the main house, in a small, charming cottage, *above*.

continued

A House with
Formal Flair
(continued)

The Kovac living room incorporates classic traditional furnishings with a fine collection of antiques, folk art, and country accessories. Many of the collectibles are housed and displayed in built-in shelves that wrap around windows on each side of the fireplace. Other prized possessions, including an outstanding collection of Imariware and Chinese export porcelain, are displayed in a distinctive early-19th-century pine cupboard, *above*. The rich red and blue colors of the porcelain are repeated in the antique rug that underscores the setting.

Although the room is basically formal in character, the blue and white "tavern check" upholstery fabric injects a pleasing touch of country flair.   *continued*

45

A plant- and flower-filled greenhouse is a pleasing adjunct to the Kovacs' kitchen dining area. With the door to the greenhouse ajar, summery fragrances waft through the room—a treat for the family during cold-weather months.

Though it looks antique, the harvest dining table is a new piece that was crafted from old wood by a local carpenter. The sausage-turned ladder-back chairs, painted deep red, also are latter-day reproductions. Even the apothecary cupboard to the left of the door is a fool-the-eye replica of an antique piece.

The only true antique in the room is the handsome (and rare) 18th-century Pennsylvania pewter dresser, *above*. Dominating one wall of the dining area, the red-painted dresser displays the Kovacs' fine collection of antique pewter, redware, and 19th-century splint baskets. The wood and tin chandelier is an 18th-century reproduction.

continued

47

A custom-made mahogany four-poster is the focal point of the Kovacs' master bedroom, *opposite*. Other handsome mahogany furnishings include the three-drawer English bachelors chest in the foreground, and the Irish Chippendale settee with its gracefully scrolled three-section back.

In true-to-tradition spirit, the bed and the windows are dressed in an authentic copy of an 18th-century resist-dyed fabric from historic Williamsburg, Virginia. This fabric, like the original, is made of high-quality cotton.

Here, as in other rooms of the Kovacs' house, the woodwork, doors, and moldings have been painted a contrasting color to accent the beautiful detailing.

An air of informal elegance pervades the guest room, *top right*. Rather than try to camouflage the quirky, odd-angled architecture, Mary Ann chose to emphasize the walls and ceiling with the lavish use of a floral striped wallpaper. For decorative unity, the twin Sheraton-style beds and the chaise longue are covered in a companion peach and green fabric.

The hallway leading to the guest room, *bottom right*, has been turned into an inviting toilette area. An English Sheraton dressing table and a Chippendale chair are fitted into a window niche that offers primpers a lovely view of the garden.

A House For Three Seasons

Though it's not winterized for year-round use, this rambling 1920s vacation house is a mecca for owners Jan and Rick McCoy. Located just a few hours' drive from the city where they live, the house is alive with family and friends on most spring and autumn weekends and all summer long. The rear of the house, with its lovely veranda and brick patio, commands a spectacular view of the salt bay beyond. Pictured *above* is a glimpse of the bay and the McCoys' boat dock, as seen from the kitchen herb garden.

continued

A House for
Three Seasons
(continued)

The McCoys are an outgoing, energetic couple who love to entertain. Parties usually are held on the terrace, but in the evening, when chilly breezes blow in from the bay, gatherings are moved indoors. Here, in the living room and the adjoining dining room, guests are treated to the comforts of a casually elegant country home.

To encourage sociability, the seating pieces—two chintz-covered armchairs, a pair of slipper chairs, and a rolled-arm sofa—are informally arranged in a semicircle. In lieu of individual end tables, the intimate grouping is served by a single coffee table covered in textured linen.

The pink and seafoam green color scheme is an appropriate choice for a summer place. The myriad colors found in the floral chintz fabric are repeated in the striped rag rug and—by happy coincidence—in the large painting on the wall behind the sofa, *above.* The window treatment is a clever *trompe l'oeil*: What looks like a fabric valance is really a wooden cornice covered with a wallpaper border.

continued

When the McCoys bought their summer place a few years ago, the present dining room was an enclosed porch. The only features of the room worth saving were the brick floor and the ceiling beams. Windows were odd-shaped and unmatched; some opened up, others opened out. Light fixtures were in all the wrong places, and the back wall, which now offers a breathtaking view, was boarded up. To remedy all these wrongs, sliding glass doors were installed to open the room to the terrace and the glorious vista. All of the mismatched windows were removed, and in their place, a new bay window (with a view of the herb garden) was installed.

Today, the remodeled porch is the most popular spot in the house. Furnished informally in a country French style, this room is where the family gathers to sip morning coffee, read the paper, or just sit around the big pine table and talk. On chilly days, a fire in the fireplace is a cozy, warming presence.

Small in Size, Big in Spirit

This small frame house in Alton, Illinois, is home for Norm and Judy Swick and their four children. When purchased 11 years ago, the house was an eyesore, inside and out. But the price was right, and the Swicks were willing to do most of the remedial work themselves.

By day, Norm is an art teacher, but his spare time is spent refinishing old furniture and creating handmade reproductions of country pieces. Judy, a nurse, is a collector of country antiques and loves to combine her finds with family heirlooms and pieces made by Norm.

The 15x34-foot living/dining area used to be two separate rooms. By removing the interior wall, the Swicks created a cozy keeping room effect. Rough plastered walls, rough sawn 8x8 cedar beams, and wooden shutters from an 1850 Pennsylvania farmhouse combine to give the room its inviting character.

Some of Norm's handmade creations include the tilt-top dining table, and the pewter shelf above the old flour bin. The Windsor chairs surrounding the table are from the state-house in Springfield, Illinois.

continued

Small in Size, Big in Spirit
(continued)

Two of the Swicks' daughters share this delightful, under-the-eaves bedroom. Norm and Judy replastered the walls, stripped and refinished the woodwork and floors, and hand-stenciled and painted the walls with patterns based on historical motifs. Placed atop the twin maple spool beds are matching honeycomb hexagonal quilts that were hand-pieced by Judy and her grandmother. The painted blanket chest between the beds is a European antique, and the charming wicker doll carriage has been pleasing little girls since it was made in 1910.

The Swicks have no place in
their lives for fads or whims.
For them, a thing is not worth
owning unless it personally connects with their lives. Their
bedroom is a beautiful expres-
sion of this belief—every object
in it is dear to their hearts. Take
the bed, for example: Though

it's a reproduction of an early
1900s piece, it has special mean-
ing, nevertheless. Norm made
the frame for the canopy, an el-
derly friend made the crocheted
canopy, and Norm's mother
crocheted the lovely spread.
    Other treasured items include
the bonnet-top cradle, the pre-

Civil War wardrobe, the walnut
mirror, and the 1860s lyre-back
rocker. Norm fashioned the cradle for their youngest child,
Nat; he also refinished the
wardrobe. The rocking chair
and mirror once belonged to
Norm's great grandparents.

New Life For an Old House

The metamorphosis of Pat and Jim Knocke's house began 130 years ago, when two small log cabins were joined as one. In 1915, a second story was added, and since then, many other changes have taken place. Today, the colonial-style exterior bears no hint of its rustic antecedents, but inside, the spirit of the past lives on.

The living room (originally one of the two log cabins) is simply but imaginatively furnished with Pat's favorite country antiques and collectibles. Serving as a sprightly, vitalizing presence in the room is the colorful plaid fabric used on the fireside wing chairs and the handsome old deacon's bench.

continued

**New Life for
An Old House**

(continued)

In the Knockes' dining room, pine and pewter team up in a warm and welcoming way. With the exception of the reproduction bow-back chairs, all of the furnishings are antique. Placed against a background of a colorful stencil-design wall covering and painted wainscot-

ing, the 1860s-vintage Welsh cupboard and the stepped-back cupboard are mellow influences in this nostalgia-evoking room. The old quilt covering the table is but one of many that Pat Knocke puts to practical and decorative use.

Although the Knockes' living room and dining room had their beginnings as log cabins, the master bedroom got its start as a screened-in porch. Both decoratively and architecturally, the room captures the countrified colonial feeling of the rest of the house. The "new" floor is made of old pine planks, and the mullioned windows were salvaged from a house slated to be torn down.

Filling the space with simple, understated beauty are the majestic mahogany highboy, the antique four-poster, and the marble-top table flanked by a pair of French-inspired armchairs. All of the furnishings are antique, as are the white cotton coverlet and the quilt at the foot of the bed. Only the crisp tieback curtains are new.

Country
Furniture

Country Furniture
Pine

The beauty of country-inspired furniture extends beyond its immediate eye appeal. Just knowing that a piece is old, that it hails from an era unlike our own, is enough to please and inspire us. But whether we're intrigued by its sentimental value or its endearing, down-home materials and design, country furniture can be counted on to enhance our surroundings and make us feel more at home.

Once considered a poor country cousin to oak, pine furniture now is a favorite of country connoisseurs and is in great demand. Its former liabilities—a plain demeanor and utilitarian styling—are now its major assets. The pine of the past is highly valued for its humble beauty and for the ease with which it mixes with other furniture styles.

Pine's popularity is not limited to the American variety. France, England, and other European countries have their own versions, and these pieces are sought after, too.

In France, provincial furniture makers turned to pine when oak became scarce in the late 1700s. French pine, with its curves, carvings, and ornamentation, closely mimics the established styles of the period. Some pieces were painted a *faux bois* (false wood) to resemble oak. Others were gussied up with white paint and gold detailing.

English country pine of the 18th and 19th centuries is straightforward, but far from primitive in either design or construction. It is handsome but uncomplicated. By the time furniture styles sifted down from the royal courts, through the aristocracy and landed gentry to country craftsmen, most of the refinements had disappeared. The designs that remained had clean lines, smooth surfaces, and simple details, qualities that are very appealing today.

Antique American pine furniture has a look of its own. Unlike French and English country furnishings that often are simplified versions of grander styles, American pine pieces are considerably more rustic in nature and, for the most part, devoid of pretense and decoration. Some early pieces were painted or stained, however. And though the vogue is for natural finishes, many country buffs are fond of old pine furnishings that exhibit traces of an original painted finish. These pieces command high prices because their numbers are relatively few.

All kinds of American country pine furnishings can be found today, although some items are harder to come by than others. Cupboards and other storage pieces in all shapes and sizes comprise the largest category of old pine furniture. Most early homes were short on storage space and cupboards took the place of closets. Some early cupboards have glass-paned doors, but most doors are solid or paneled.

Pine chests were extremely popular for the storage of linens, woolens, and quilts. And these early pine pieces are just as functional today as they were when they were first made.

Other popular storage pieces include pie safes and dry sinks. Pie safes were used in the kitchen for the storage of foodstuffs. Their pierced tin panels (often elaborately designed) allowed for air circulation while deterring the intrusion of insects and small animals. Small versions of pie safes were suspended from rafters and were pulled up and down by a rope. This conserved floor space and kept the contents safe.

Pine dry sinks were used in the kitchen for holding washbasins and buckets of water. The forerunner of the dry sink was the bucket bench—an open set of shelves used to store kitchen necessities.

It isn't necessary to buy antique pine to appreciate its beauty in your home. New pine furnishings such as the chairs pictured here offer the same natural woody warmth and homey vintage styling as their antique counterparts.

Made in about 1800, this freestanding corner cabinet is typical of the unadorned, utilitarian styling favored by the Pennsylvania Dutch. In wealthy homes, cabinets usually were built into the room.

This handsome American version of the popular European blanket chest features two bottom drawers and a lift-up top. Brass hardware adds a touch of elegance.

Although American-made about 1820, this monk's bench (also known as a chair table) is a 15th-century design. The multifunctional monk's bench came to the New World with the Pilgrims and was quite popular in American homes for another 200 years. Originals are rare and expensive.

English And Irish Pine

The countrified English regency corner cabinet originally was a built-in with a concave barrel back. Style and condition affect the value of these cabinets more than age does.

Placed atop a chest of drawers, a bedding box like this 1850s version was a staple in country bedrooms. Similar grain and a good fit between the units indicated a matched set. "Married" pieces, those made at different times and combined later, usually cost less.

More than a mere bench, this 1760 Irish settle folded out to make a bed-in-a-box for farm families and guests. Most settles were made of oak, with storage space located under a hinged seat. This pine settle is rare.

Irish pine, more than English, often featured cutout details. This Irish dresser (where food was "dressed" before serving) mimics, in a ruralized way, the English Regency style of the period. The sleigh feet are a bonus.

French Pine

The most elegant of all pine furnishings are pieces made by the French. This flower-adorned early-19th-century marriage armoire is a fine example of country craftsmanship. Marriage armoires were made to order by the bride's parents, then filled with linens for the new household.

Not all country French pine is ornate. By the mid-1800s, excessive curves and carvings gave way to rectilinear lines like those of this stately buffet from the French province of Bordeaux.

72

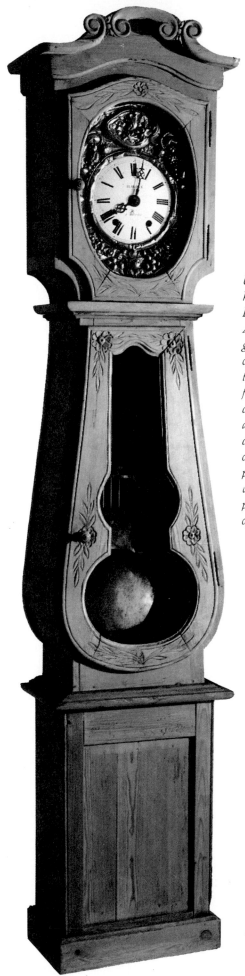

Unlike the handsome but boxy English- and American-made grandfather clocks of the early 1800s, those from France featured curved cabinets, carvings, and elaborate crowns. This clock originally was painted white, as was much French provincial furniture of the time.

This early 19th-century bonnetière was designed originally for the storage of large plumed hats. Today, French pine bonnetières like this beauty function as armoires.

Oak

Oak furniture reached its peak of popularity between 1880 and 1915. It was at this time that the industrial revolution took furniture-making out of the hands of artisans and into the realm of factory mass production. For the first time, the public had access to soundly constructed furniture that was readily available at affordable prices. Much of this old oak furniture survives today, and there are many varieties to choose from.

Golden oak

This term is almost synonymous with turn-of-the-century oak furniture, most of which was made of white oak. For time- and cost-saving reasons, most of these mass-produced pieces were left unstained and free of elaborate adornment. Instead, manufacturers applied several light coats of a slightly yellowish varnish to enhance the light and dark brown tones of the beautiful wood. The resulting color effect gave rise to the term "golden oak."

Quarter-sawn or tiger oak

These terms were used interchangeably to describe the highest quality oak lumber in use between 1880 and 1915. Furniture-grade oak logs were cut lengthwise at right angles to

the tree's growth rings to expose more of the dark grain of the wood. The alternating light and dark patterns looked like the stripes of a tiger (detail A).

Quarter-sawing (detail B) was anything but efficient and much of the log was turned into sawdust in the process. But because oak lumber was so plentiful at the time, furniture makers didn't give much thought to conservation. As the great forests thinned, however, the practice became less common.

After 1915, some factories covered inferior wood with oak veneer, a thin sheet of better wood peeled from the log and glued to tabletops and drawer fronts. Often, age and humidity caused the glue to deteriorate and the veneer to warp and

crack. Because of oak's popularity, price differences between veneered and non-veneered oak furniture are minimal.

Fumed oak

Some oak furniture, particularly pieces made after 1900, was deliberately darkened by exposing it to ammonia fumes. The unfinished item was placed in an airtight box along with saucers of ammonia. As the liquid evaporated, its fumes caused a chemical reaction that turned the wood brown. The degree of darkening was controlled by the amount of ammonia and the length of time the furniture was left in the box.

Today, the least expensive old oak furniture can be found at secondhand stores and auctions, but often the wood is hidden beneath layers of paint. To see if the piece is really oak, look for unpainted places on the bottom, back, or inside drawers.

Refinishing oak is fairly easy because its hardness will stand up to strong paint removers and putty knives. However, avoid using sandpaper or water-rinse removers; both can raise the grain and will make the job much tougher. Use fine-grade steel wool instead. One more pointer: Don't take oak furniture to a place that strips it by dipping it in a vat of chemicals. The process can bleach out the color, loosen joints, and cause the wood to swell and split.

Oak pedestal tables are still easy to find. This example accommodates two extra leaves.

Simple and honest in design and construction, this

golden oak washstand is typical of the popular Eastlake style.

The Arts and Crafts Movement of the early 1900s produced a style of furniture known as "mission oak." Handcrafted by artisans (in revolt to the machine age), the furniture, as illustrated by these pieces, was durable, functional, and devoid of frills.

The shallow relief design on the back of this high chair was pressed by machine, not hand carved. All types of furnishings were produced with this ersatz decoration, and many examples can be found today.

The designs of many old oak pieces are quirky and original. This 1926 ladies desk, with a style of its own, features fancy scrolling, applied wood carvings, cabriole legs, and hoof feet.

Country Furniture
Miscellaneous Woods

Many types of wood were used in the construction of country furniture, not just oak and pine. Availability and suitability to function determined the choice of wood. Depending on where you live, you're apt to come across furniture made of birch, maple, walnut, cherry, or poplar.

Made of birch, this well-proportioned drop-leaf table, circa 1810-1830, hails from New England.

Round worktables are quite rare, and this one, made mostly of maple, probably was used in an 1840s tavern or inn. Of interest are the Sheraton-style legs: Two are made of maple, and two are of walnut.

This one-drawer poplar table, a rural interpretation of Hepplewhite styling, is charming and endearing in its naiveté.

Sturdy and substantial, this walnut plank farm table was made in Missouri during the last quarter of the 19th century. It features a top that lifts off for cleaning.

Constructed of cherry, this handcrafted country cupboard is as functional today as it was when it was built 125 years ago. Note the wide backboards: They're indicative of early (pre-20th-century) styling.

Country Furniture
Painted and Stenciled

Many early pieces of country furniture were either painted or stenciled. One function of paint was surface protection; another was to hide the fact that a piece might have been constructed of "lesser" woods. About 1815, stenciled furniture made its appearance. The man who popularized stenciled furniture was Lambert Hitchcock. His chair designs are still very popular today.

Slant-top desks were made in all areas of the country during the 19th century. This one, with its original red-painted finish and brass hardware, was probably a schoolmaster's desk.

This painted and stenciled 1840 Windsor chair is an example of American folk art. The painted green circles on the legs, stretchers, and spindled back are imitations of bamboo turnings.

What elevates this 1889 pine blanket box from the ordinary is the grain painting on the sides and top. Because it is signed and dated, the chest likely was made for a special occasion.

Grain painting was very fashionable in the 19th century. It was a fanciful attempt to imitate the graining of high-style woods such as burled mahogany and rosewood, but the results usually bear little resemblance to the real thing. The grain-painted handiwork on this 1889 cupboard was achieved with combs and sponges.

Half-round tables are something of a rarity, and this rough-crafted example is rarer yet because it retains its original blue paint. In typical primitive fashion, the two-board top is simply nailed to the deep apron below.

Few early rural craftsmen had the time, inclination, or ability to construct fine, intricately styled furniture. The simplest forms usually were made in an uncomplicated manner for an immediate and specific need. However, even the most primitive, crudely fashioned furnishings have a flair and subtle charm of their own. Indeed, it is the absence of sophistication that makes primitive furniture so appealing to collectors today.

During the early 1800s, one day a week was set aside for the purpose of baking bread. Dough boxes like this one were used for mixing ingredients. After mixing, the box would be moved to a warm place so the dough could rise.

The primitive appeal of this cupboard lies in its rugged, strictly functional air. Constructed of wide pine planks, the piece originally was used as a canning cupboard and even has notations referring to its contents penciled on an inside door.

Children's furniture from the late 18th and early 19th centuries is very special. This lilliputian chair, no doubt lovingly made by a proud father, features a splinted hickory seat, tiny finials, and sturdy arms terminating in turned front posts. The original red paint covers the various types of wood used in the chair's construction.

Caring for Country Furniture

The beauty and value of old and antique furniture is largely dependent on how well the piece has been cared for over the years. Given proper attention, prized country furnishings will last—and look good—for generations to come.

Check the finish first

When selecting a cleaning method, the type of finish is more important than the kind of wood. A satiny shellac finish, for example, may dissolve if cleaned with a product that contains alcohol or turpentine. A cream polish is fine for a varnished surface, but it will make a waxed finish gummy and dull.

No matter what the finish, all furniture benefits from occasional dusting to keep grit from settling into the carvings and pores. To remove dust from crevices or elaborately carved areas, use a brush covered with a slightly damp cloth.

Cleaning varnished wood

Antique dealers and museum caretakers often use a mild solution of *soap and water* to remove accumulations of dirt and grime from varnished wood furniture,

but this method should be used with caution. Too much water can loosen glue joints, so work with a sponge that's damp only, never wet. *Caution*: Soap and water should not be used at all on veneered or inlaid wood, or on pieces finished with shellac or lacquer.

To create your own cleaning solution, mix one teaspoon of mild powder soap with a quart of lukewarm water. (Don't use heavy-duty soap or products designed for cleaning woodwork or floors.)

Before working with water, test a small, inconspicuous area of the wood. If the surface turns milky white, do not use this method of cleaning. Otherwise, proceed by dipping a soft cloth (or sponge) in the mixture, squeezing the cloth almost dry, then gently washing a small area at a time. Rinse the piece with a cloth slightly dampened with clear warm water, then dry thoroughly with a clean soft cloth. Move to an adjacent area to repeat the process. Let the

furniture air-dry for 24 hours before rewaxing.

Chemical-based cleaning products such as mineral spirits or synthetic turpentine also can be used on varnished surfaces. Used in the same way as a soap and water solution, these products dissolve dirt and grease without softening the finish.

Apply the products with a soft cloth or sponge. Use a small stiff-bristled brush on places where dirt clings. Rinse with fresh liquid, wipe with a clean cloth, and let the furniture dry for 24 hours.

Combining methods. If a piece of furniture is caked with grime, some antique owners use both cleaning methods, starting with a gentle washing and following with a cleaning product intended for varnished wood.

If you choose a combination method, give the piece a mild soap and water sponging (with the sponge almost dry), rinse carefully, then dry. After the piece has dried, rub the surface with 000 or 0000 steel wool soaked in synthetic turpentine. The solvent removes the grease, and the fine steel wool removes loose dirt without harming the surface. Wipe the treated area with a clean cloth, dampened with turpentine, to remove steel wool particles.

Cleaning lacquered and painted finishes

To remove dull film from a lacquered piece, use a homemade paste of flour and olive oil. Apply the paste with a soft, clean cloth, rubbing with a circular motion. Wipe the paste off, then polish the surface with a soft material such as women's hosiery. Never use water on a lacquered finish.

Mild soap and warm water are most commonly used on painted wood finishes. Too much water, however, wets the wood and tends to lift the paint off the surface. Be sure to work with extreme care. Use cleaning cloths that are soft and free of any abrasive grit. Wring the cloth nearly dry, then wash a small section at a time. Rinse with a second cloth dampened with clear water. Dry thoroughly with a clean cloth. Avoid using linseed oil cleaners; they tend to darken and discolor painted surfaces.

Polishing

There is no miracle polish that is right for every wood finish, but a hard carnauba paste wax polish is the most versatile. It gives a protective finish that fends off fingerprints and doesn't attract dust.

Initially, paste wax requires considerably more work to apply than a liquid polish does, but, eventually, a hard, lustrous surface will develop, and then the upkeep is reduced to an occasional waxing.

Fine antique furniture made of hardwoods such as walnut, mahogany, rosewood, fruitwood, and maple should be waxed sparingly every six months. Hand-rubbing the piece is the secret to bringing out the beauty of the wood.

Country pine, poplar, and oak often have oil finishes. These types of woods should be touched up periodically with a mixture of equal parts of vinegar, turpentine, and boiled linseed oil. Simply rub on the oil dressing with a dampened cloth. After several hours, wipe off any excess.

Cane and wicker

If your furniture has cane inserts, these can be cleaned with mild soap and warm water. Dip a sponge into the sudsy solution, squeeze it nearly dry, then wipe the cane carefully. Rinse with clean water; dry thoroughly with a clean cloth.

To clean natural unpainted wicker, wash it with a solution of one cup of peroxide and one cup of vinegar combined in a five-gallon pail of water. Apply with a sponge, rinse with clean water, and let dry thoroughly.

Painted wicker should be dusted regularly with a damp rag. To clean, use a sponge and clear water, being careful not to soak and damage the paint.

Cleaning brass hardware

The real secret to shiny brass is in the polishing, and that means applying plenty of old-fashioned elbow grease.

Remember, the brass polish can stain a wood finish, so, if possible, remove the hardware before cleaning.

Noncommercial cleaners also may be used on brass. Mix a solution of salt and vinegar. Or, rub brass pieces with a mixture of very fine sand and water.

Country
Touches

Country Touches
Rag Rugs

When all is said and done, it's the finishing touches that bring a country scheme into focus. Rugs, fabrics, window treatments, wall coverings, light fixtures, and accessories are among the extras that imbue a room with style and personality.

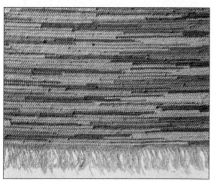

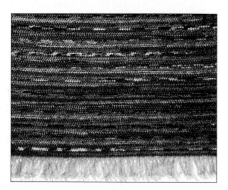

Colorful rag rugs and woven rugs, like those used by our pioneer ancestors, always can be counted on to enhance a country-style decor. Some versions, like the handmade cotton pastel rugs, *opposite*, are right at home in contemporary settings. Just as striking are the textured, hand-woven beauties pictured *above*.

Random patterns saved time and effort and often were used by pioneer weavers. The two versions shown *at left* are made of wool.

Plain-weave, solid-color rugs like the blue cotton rug *at top right* also are available, and they come in many sizes.

Also pictured *at right* are two runners—one done in a contemporary checkerboard design, the other in a multicolor plaid.

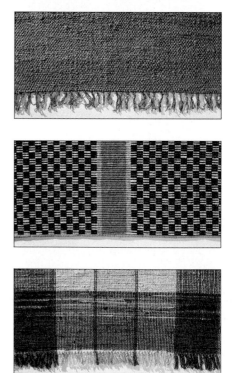

Country Touches
Hooked Rugs

Early makers of hooked rugs, though unschooled in the fine arts, found plenty of design inspiration in their everyday surroundings. Now, as then, primitive, naïve designs are the most visually satisfying.

Just about any hooked rug makes an apt foundation for a country decor, and many, like the Schoolhouse Quilt rug, *top right,* are worthy of hanging on the wall as artwork.

Pictured *opposite* is a hand-hooked wool "patch" rug that blends the best of contemporary colors with an age-old pattern.

The delightful "Pigs in Clover" rug, *center left,* is an example of a whimsical primitive design motif. Another popular old folk art motif, the horse, is depicted in the small, hand-hooked rug, *bottom left.*

Floral-pattern hooked rugs are apt choices for formal settings. The handsome oval area rug, *center right*, is all wool, and has a Victorian air to it.

The "Sanford Antique" rug, *bottom right*, is an adaptation of a very old rug originally made by Ralph Burnam, who was known as the king of hooked rugs in the early 1900s.

Country Touches
Braided Rugs

L ong considered common-
place because they were so
easy to make, braided rugs
today are enjoying a revival.
The six examples pictured here
all would be decorative assets in
a down-home country setting.

The colors of the thick,
nubby rug, *opposite*, are reminiscent of the vibrant blues and
barn reds so popular in old
painted country furniture. This
4x6 oval is made of wool.

Adding cheer and charm to a
farmhouse porch, *top right*, is a
braided beauty made of old-
fashioned calico fabric.

Heart-shape rugs are special
symbols of the past, and are
still much-loved today. This
pink, blue, and purple example,
center left, would make a beautiful "welcome" in an entryway.

Rugs made of wool or wool
blends feel wonderful under-
foot. The oval area rug *at bottom
left* is braided in soft, pretty
wool pastels, and would be a
smart choice for a child's room.

Braided rugs come in an infi-
nite variety of sizes, shapes, and
patterns. For old-time appeal,
look for a flat-braided rug like
the one pictured *center right*. For
a more sophisticated homespun
look, try a random-pattern
braided rug such as the one
shown *at bottom right.*

Fabric

O f all the embellishments that one can choose for a country-style room, fabric offers the greatest decorative potential. There are literally thousands of patterns, prints, and color combinations to cull from, and today, many yard goods designs (and sheets, too) are sold in conjunction with coordinating wall coverings and stylish window treatments—a real boon for the indecisive.

Fabric's major asset is its versatility. Just a few yards can go miles in setting the style and personality of a room, or adding new vitality to a dated scheme. Whether used for slipcovers, toss pillows, or table skirts, well-chosen fabrics can be counted on to offer immediate, eye-catching results.

Still another asset of fabric is cost. Many of the most captivating country prints are amazingly inexpensive. Delightful cottons, cotton blends, chintzes, muslins, and linens abound, and one needn't search long before a good buy is found. Indeed, it's not always necessary to shop in stores. Today, there are many shop-by-mail companies from which to order country yard goods and readymades.

To see a small sampling of charming fabric prints and patterns available today, just turn the page. *continued*

Fabric
(continued)

When selecting fabric for a country scheme, keep in mind that different patterns and prints have varying effects on a room. Large floral motifs, for instance, tend to visually domi- nate a room. As a general rule, large or bold color prints and patterns are best reserved for fairly spacious rooms; small, delicate patterns are most effec- tive in relatively small spaces.

Small Floral Prints

Large Floral Prints

American Country Coordinates

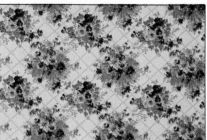

French Country Border

Small-Dot Prints

Country Touches
Windows

Few things emphasize the decorating style of a room more than window treatments do, but all too often they're afterthoughts. This is unfortunate because the right choice of treatment will enhance not only the decor, but the view and the room's architecture as well. The wrong window treatment, on the other hand, can detract from an otherwise appealing scheme.

When it comes to choosing country-inspired window treatments, the choices are many and varied. Narrowing the possibilities is mostly a matter of analyzing a room's character. Some treatments naturally lend themselves to simple, understated schemes, others to cozy, down-home settings, and still others to gracious and formal surrounds. Frills and flounces will make one kind of statement; simple shutters or shades, another.

Keep in mind, too, the size, shape, and location of the window when considering treatment options. Skimpy curtains look inappropriate on tall, stately windows, and heavy draperies are apt to overpower a small window. And, if you're fortunate enough to have a window that affords a spectacular view, take pains not to cover it up.

Lace curtains often conjure up images of a gracious past. You can recapture the aura of those days with beautiful laces like these ready-made curtains, or sew your own, using lace purchased by the yard.

continued

Window Shopping

Whether in the form of softly pleated draperies or breezy, billowy curtains, fabric window treatments are the first choice of most country decorating fans. Curtains of calico, gingham, lace, flowered prints, dotted swiss, stripes, checks, and plaids are among the perennial old-fashioned favorites. Popular, too, are treatments embellished with fringe, scalloped edges, ruffles, ribbon, embroidery, and stencil designs.

Fabric coverings range from minimal to maximal in terms of privacy, light control, and energy-saving qualities, and can be purchased custom-made, ready-made, made-to-order from stores, or through a variety of mail order firms. Generally, custom window treatments are the most costly, readymades and mail order treatments the least. Home-sewn treatments can offer the biggest savings of all.

Other country-style window treatments worth considering are louvered wood shutters, woven-wood shades, wide-vane plantation shutters, and pouf shades. Certain spring-roller shades, especially if they're laminated with fabric or a stencil motif, also look great in a country setting.

The most ordinary window in the world can gain distinction, charm, and style with the simple addition of a window treatment.

To prove the point, we've taken a standard double-hung sash window and transformed its plain personality in nine winning ways.

Wooden shutters adapt beautifully to just about any type of decor, but they look particularly charming in cottage-style rooms.

Louvered shutters offer privacy and light control at the flick of a wrist. Unfinished shutters can be painted or left as is.

Informal elegance is provided by side panel curtains *that cascade to the floor. These heavy cotton, large-scale floral print curtains are lined in cotton* sateen, *and are hung from wooden rings on a natural-finish pine pole. The rush-seat chair is a countrified version of a Queen Anne design.*

Unpretentious cafe curtains *in calico or gingham are always at home in country decors. Though they're seen most often in kitchens and* bathrooms, they can be used in any casual setting. Some treatments are done tier over tier, but this one is topped with a matching shirred valance.

Delicate lace curtains *call up images of an old-world era and make beautiful adjuncts to Victorian and country French* settings. Use readymade panels like these, or sew your own, using antique remnants or lace purchased by the yard.

Embroidered tambour curtains *usually are made of cotton batiste—a sheer handkerchief-like material. Their lightweight, breezy* qualities make them popular window treatments during the warm-weather months.

The simple styling *of* tab curtains *makes them excellent choices for understated country schemes. They're usually made of* cotton or homespun, and look best when hung on poles placed above the window frame.

Old-fashioned romantic appeal is provided by this shirred swag and half-curtain treatment trimmed in ball fringe. Just about any fabric can be used for a cascading swag-over-tier covering, but chintz, calico, and plain cotton look best.

Quaint and charming priscilla curtains *are undoubtedly the most popular of all country window treatments. Placed within the window* frame, this semi-sheer pair is gracefully trimmed, front and bottom, with a self ruffle and matching fabric tiebacks.

For many people, priscillas *aren't really priscillas unless they're adorned with frills and flounces. This lavish treatment breaks on the floor* and features a shirred valance sewn right into the delicate rosebud-print curtains.

Country Touches
Wall Coverings

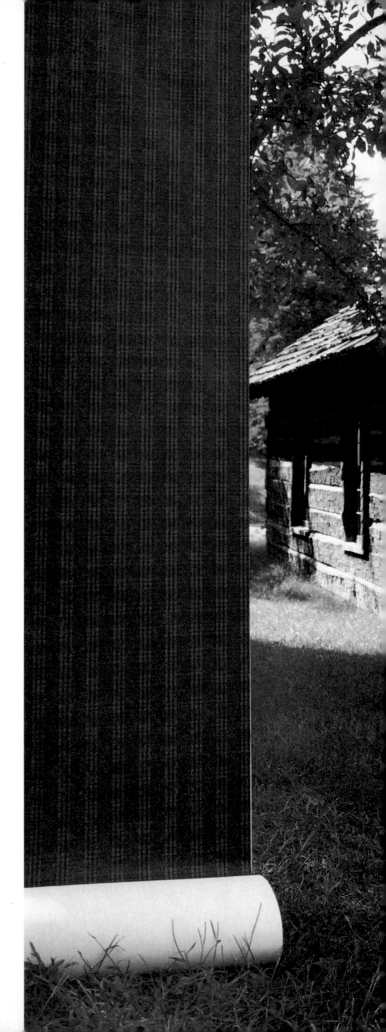

The biggest problem in selecting a wall covering for a country-style room is narrowing the myriad choices. The marketplace abounds with wall covering possibilities in every conceivable pattern and print. Motifs, including borders, run the gamut from delightfully delicate miniprints to large-scale floral designs bursting in colorful bloom. Other prints that are big in country character include trellis patterns, regimented dots, stripes, and tavern checks.

In recent years, documented historical prints have become widely available. Collections of wall coverings endorsed by prestigious American museums and respected restoration villages such as Greenfield Village, Michigan, can be found at wall covering outlets and retail stores, and through interior designers. Many historical prints are authentic reproductions— exact copies of an original print in terms of color, scale, pattern, and width. Prints that have been modified in one way or another are called adaptations.

If you'd like to learn more about the history of wall coverings and see one of the finest collections of period papers in America, visit the Cooper-Hewitt Museum, 2 East 91st Street, New York, NY 10028. If a visit isn't possible, write for the museum's list of publications on wall coverings, period wall-covering sources, or companies that specialize in cleaning and restoring antique coverings.

continued

102

Wall Coverings
(continued)

The wall-covering patterns shown here represent but a small fraction of the thousands of styles available. Kinds of coverings range from machine-printed and hand-printed papers to vinyls, grass cloth, and fabrics. Some coverings are prepasted, strippable, scrubbable, and washable, but better papers usually are not scrubbable. Be sure to check these factors.

Trellis Variations

Petite Florals

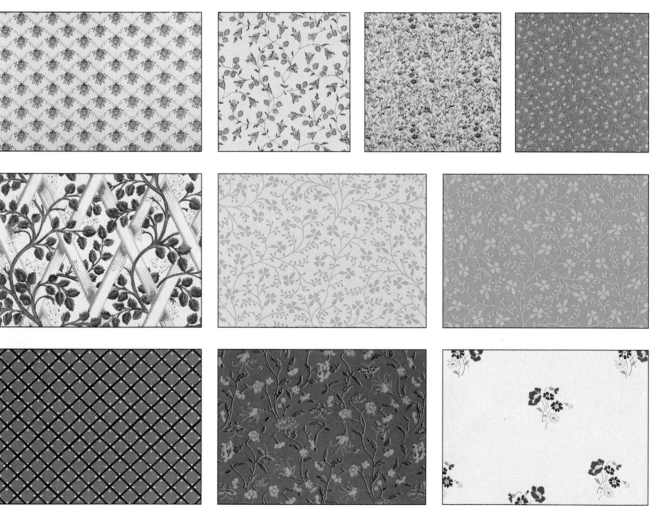

Regimented Dots

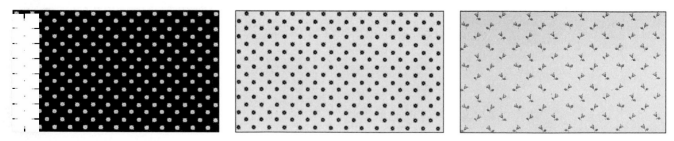

Allover Floral

Variations in Stripes

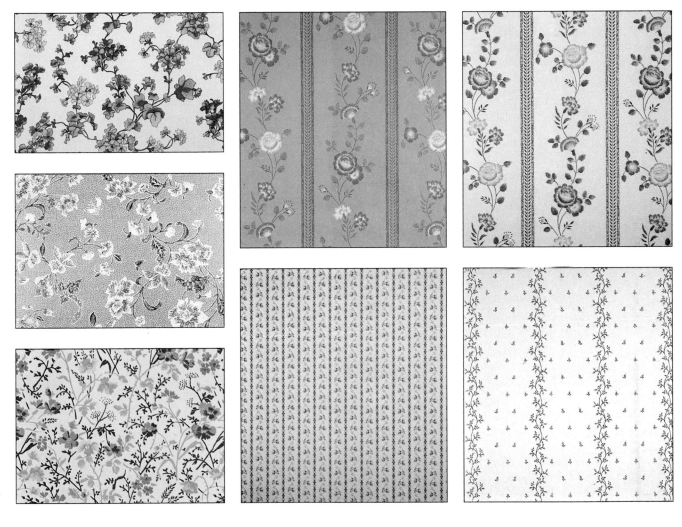

Stencil Design

Wallpaper Borders

Country Touches
All Kinds of Accents

A major part of the fun and enjoyment of putting together a country decorating scheme comes from finishing off the room with eye-catching accents and accessories. Much of the pleasure comes in the looking. A true country connoisseur never tires of seeking out treasures. Nearly every city and small town in America boasts at least one "country shop" or antique store that's brimming with items of interest. And stores aren't the only sources. Crafts fairs, flea markets, collectors' shows, and auctions also are meccas for the country accessories shopper.

The vignette pictured here features a miscellany of charming accessories designed to add character to country settings. Some accessory items are primarily whimsical in nature—the ceramic duck teapot, the painted block houses, and the sheep handcrafted of wood and string are examples. Many accents are as useful as they are enchanting. Included in this category are the wrought-iron sausage rack that's been turned into an animal ring chandelier, the pierced-tin table lamp, the hand-painted tiles, the electrified French oil lamp, and the assortment of delightful print wallpapers and borders shown here.

Country
Collections

Redware and Yellowware

Collecting things of country origin is the favorite pastime of many people, and it's easy to understand why. America of bygone days offers us a rich and fascinating heritage of decorative, functional, and just-for-fun objects to enjoy and admire in our homes. If you're a newcomer to the world of country collectibles, keep in mind that the items we've selected to show you here represent but a small sampling of what await you at antique shops, auctions, and flea markets.

Redware represents the earliest form of American pottery and is prized by collectors today. First made in colonial New England and Pennsylvania, redware was produced for kitchen and tabletop use. The term "redware" is somewhat misleading because not all pieces are actually red in color. Though the clay itself was typically red, minerals added to the glazes produced a variety of striking colors. In New England, for example, manganese often was added to create a shiny black glaze. Iron oxide produced a bright orange glaze; copper turned the pottery green.

In Pennsylvania, a yellow decoration called "slipware" was commonly used. In this process, a slip mixture of water, finely ground clay, powdery lead, and other minerals was poured, brushed, or dribbled over the pottery to produce a special design or lettering effect.

Because few, if any, pieces were produced after the year 1900, true redware pottery decorated in the traditional manner is scarce. However, undecorated, strictly utilitarian pieces such as crocks are in better supply. Color, decoration, and rarity determine price. Although it was originally designed for functional use, redware—because of its fragile nature—is best limited to decorative use.

Unlike redware, yellowware is quite sturdy, and thus, in greater supply today. Yellowware was first produced in the 1830s from a unique Ohio clay that turned a dull yellow when fired. By the late 19th century, many forms of yellowware were being made. The most popular pieces were sets of mixing bowls, ranging in size from two to 24 inches wide. The challenge for today's collector is to acquire a complete set. Other desirable pieces include rolling pins, pudding molds, and pie plates.

Displayed on and around an old table, *right,* is a prized collection of red- and yellowware. Any one of these crafted pieces would serve handsomely in a home as a colorful and functional reminder of the past.

Enamelware

Enamelware is a catchall word for an assortment of household items made of iron or steel and coated with a shiny, porcelainlike glaze. The process was developed in the 1700s, but it wasn't until after the Civil War that American companies started mass producing enamelware articles for kitchens and bathrooms. Other terms used for enamelware include graniteware, agateware, and porcelain ware (these were trade names of the day).

The turn-of-the-century housewife applauded enamelware for its smooth, easy-to-clean surface. It was relatively lightweight, not harmed by acidic foods, and more cheerful than drab tin and cast-iron kitchenware. Fragility was its only disadvantage. Subject to constant wear, pie plates and dishpans were always getting chipped. Once the enamel covering wore off, the metal soon rusted through. When this happened, the thrifty housewife would rejuvenate the worn-out piece with "Mendits"—small metal plugs sold to repair enamelware pots and pans.

The decline of this once-popular, ubiquitous product came with the introduction of aluminum cookware in the 1920s and the closing of factories during the Great Depression.

Many items to choose from

Although not of great investment potential, enamelware is affordable and easy to find in all parts of the country at auctions, flea markets, and antique shops. Its real charm, however, lies in its diversity of color, size, and shape; you needn't be an avid collector to enjoy its presence in your home.

Items you're likely to come across include everyday household articles such as cooking utensils, pitchers, bowls, plates, and washbasins. With a bit of luck, you might happen upon an enamelware kitchen stove, icebox, kitchen table, or sink that's still in good condition.

Among the hard-to-find collector's items are enamelware canister sets, salt boxes, utensil racks, miniatures, preserve jars, rolling pins, water coolers, and butter churns. Other sought-after pieces include enamelware trimmed in pewter, cast iron, and wood.

Features to look for

Color and condition are the main features to look for when appraising enamelware. Solid gray and gray and white are the most plentiful shades in enamelware, but blue is prevalent, too. Less common colors are red, purple, brown, green, and pink. Plain white pieces with enameled figures or lettering are rarer yet. Least common of all are pieces exhibiting a lithographed decoration. Most enamelware is chipped or dented as a result of use and age, and unless the damage is severe, the dents needn't be considered detrimental to the piece.

Another clue to age (besides wear) is heaviness. Generally, the earlier pieces are quite heavy. A featherlight piece probably is not old—in fact, because enamelware still is being manufactured today, a lightweight item may well be brand new. Should you come across an enamelware comb case, chamber pot, or meat grinder, the piece most likely is old.

If you purchase an old piece of enamelware that is in need of cleaning, do it gently. Don't scrub with an abrasive cleaner or pad. Oven cleaner works well to remove grime. To remove stains from the inside of the cookware, try this home remedy: Boil peeled potatoes in the stained vessel. Except for cleaning and treating any exposed metal to a light rubbing of cooking oil, the item should be left as is.

Pictured *opposite* is an assortment of enamelware in many shapes and forms. Most of the items are representative of what you're apt to come across at auctions and antique shops, but the blue porcelain-coated iron parlor stove, and the pewter-trimmed teapot (sitting atop a colander) are both rare finds.

Spatterware And Spongeware

Spatterware is a style of decoration rather than an actual type of pottery. Applied to many types of light clay kitchenware in the 18th and 19th centuries, spatter decoration got its start as an inexpensive alternative to fine European and English pottery. Created for mass appeal, it was bright, cheery, and unsophisticated. Belying its humble origins, spatterware today is a highly popular collector's item.

Several basic types of spatter decoration exist. True spatter is recognizable by a design of closely patterned dots forming a border around a single motif. Another type of spatter design is known as sesign. It is characterized by structured, small-shape designs set close together but with a lighter, airier appearance than true spatter.

Still another type of spatterware is cut sponge or stamped ware. A smooth sponge was cut into a design shape, dipped into paint color, then applied to the ware, producing a design that was repeated many times.

Painted center motifs in all types of spatterware include houses, floral designs, peafowl, roosters, and stars. Border designs also are varied; they include floral designs, horseshoes, holly, bow knots, and geometric patterns. Some spatterware decoration features transfer patterns, eagles, rabbits, and scenic designs.

Determining the age of spatterware is somewhat difficult because the same patterns were produced for many years, and many of the early pieces were unmarked. One clue to age is the piece itself. Handleless cups, for instance, rarely were made after 1860.

Spongeware

Spongeware is a term used to describe a thick, sturdy, and substantial pottery used in the preparation of food and for general household use. Bowls, pitchers, mugs, pots, and, occasionally, strainers are the most commonly found pieces.

The body of spongeware is somewhat porous but covered with a heavy, durable glaze. As the term implies, spongeware decoration looks sponged. Frequently there is no specific design, just an overall pattern, sparse and closely set.

The most common color of spongeware is blue. Cobalt or dark blue is seen most often, but lighter blues can be found, too. Less common colors are green, brown, yellow, and red.

Sometimes, two or three colors were applied to one piece, one over the other, to create a variegated look. Few pieces of spongeware have additional decoration other than the sponge effect itself.

As with other types of antiques, rarity, condition, and age affect the value of spongeware. Damaged items usually are shunned by collectors, except when the item is of great rarity, or if it fills a gap in a collection.

Pictured *opposite* is a mid-19th-century cupboard filled with a colorful miscellany of spatterware and spongeware. On the top shelf is a group of plates, cups, and saucers with simple blue spatter borders. Below, three cut-sponge plates in a flower and foliage pattern stand behind three similar handleless cups. A large sugar bowl in a pink and blue swag spatter is displayed beside them. On the center shelf, a spatter cake plate with a thistle center motif stands behind two handleless spatter cups. To the left of these is a small pale blue and white sponge pitcher with white banding at the top and bottom edges. To the right, a large pitcher displays dark cobalt blue sponge decoration. A sponge chamber pot and a shallow mixing bowl share the bottom shelf.

Country Collections
Majolica

It wasn't until the late 1800s that Majolica was made in America. The name "Majolica" refers to a type of highly colorful tin-glazed pottery that originally was made in the Balearic Islands, the largest of which is Majorca. Similar types of pottery were developed in various European countries, but it's 19th-century American-made Majolica that became the rage in this country for many years.

Three European potteries—Palissy, Whieldon, and Wedgwood—were the forerunners of American earthenware Majolica. Instead of using opaque tin glazes, these potteries relied upon transparent lead glazes that were cheaper than tin to produce, and also allowed the use of more brilliant, accurate colors than those found on their tin-glazed counterparts.

Most 19th-century Majolica was molded in naturalistic shapes, stacked in boxes, and fired in a kiln. Interestingly, the decoration process was done almost exclusively by young women. Working in factories, they produced literally hundreds of forms and shapes for both decorative and utilitarian use. Some of the more common design motifs are corn, maple leaf, begonia, bamboo, shell, geranium, as well as dozens of animals and birds. Two designs that were plentiful and distinctly American were begonia leaf and corn. Begonia leaf plates come in all sizes and colors, some with a handle.

For the most part, early American Majolica was not marked. American potteries, in an attempt to compete with the imports, copied English designs and sold them for less money than authentic imported Majolica. Many English potteries, including Wedgwood, Minton, and G. Jones, did mark their works. One important exception is Whieldon, 1740-1780. His pottery, characterized by tortoise shell glazes, is now quite rare and expensive.

With Majolica, there is always a question of whether to purchase damaged items. Most antique dealers insist on perfect pieces, but it is extremely rare to find American Majolica without some signs of wear. Soft pottery covered with hard glazes is very susceptible to cracking and crazing, and not many pieces remain unscathed. Generally, only pieces used solely for show are likely to have escaped wear and damage.

An eye-catching Majolica collection such as the one pictured here can still be found with diligent searching and careful buying. But, as this colorful pottery continues to increase in value, and as collectors become more and more plentiful, Majolica is becoming increasingly scarce.

Stoneware

For the people who lived in 19th-century rural America, stoneware crocks and jugs were not collector's items, but purely functional containers for the storage of foodstuffs. In fact, it wasn't until the 1960s, when redware and other early pottery became quite expensive, that stoneware entered the collectibles arena. Today, stoneware is appreciated for its simple, straightforward shapes, and its delightful, naïve decoration.

Unlike other forms of pottery whose glazes are applied before firing, stoneware was glazed in a kiln and fired at a temperature of more than 2000 degrees Fahrenheit. Salt was shoveled into the hot kiln containing the pottery. As it vaporized, a fine mist covered the pottery, producing a hard, transparent surface with a slight texture called salt glaze. This firing technique created a product that was exceptionally hard and durable—explaining why so much stoneware survives today.

Many different forms of stoneware were produced, but the types most commonly seen today are jugs and crocks. Among the most desirable (and uncommon) stoneware items are ovoid jugs. Made from the late 1700s until the 1840s, the ovoid is easily recognizable by its broad top tapering down to a narrow base. From the mid-1800s to the early 1900s, jugs gradually became less ovoid and more straight-sided in shape.

Stoneware crocks have wide mouths and were used as preserving and canning jars. Designed to be sealed with wax, string, or stoneware lids, they gradually were replaced in the late 19th century by glass preserve jars.

Other forms of stoneware that may be found today include spittoons, pitchers, bowls, and miniature items.

Most stoneware items are decorated in either cobalt oxide or manganese. Cobalt oxide produces a blue ornamentation; manganese produces a brown or black decoration.

In determining the value of stoneware, decoration as well as form is very important. Charming, unstudied motifs, including flowers, birds, animals, buildings, and human figures, were applied by hand. The less common of these are considered folk art. Later period crocks and jugs frequently were stenciled in cobalt, a process that took less time than hand slip-trailed decoration. These pieces are less valuable than hand-decorated stoneware items.

In addition to their decoration, most early stoneware pieces are marked by the potter's name. Also, a number—1, 2, 3, for example—often is found, indicating the jug or crock's capacity in gallons.

Hairline cracks, chips, and flaking on decorated stoneware are detrimental to the value of the item. However, rarity in a piece may diminish the importance of slight damage or wear.

Displayed in the mid-19th-century chimney cupboard *at right* are various forms of decorated stoneware. On top of the cupboard is a lug-handled, straight-sided crock with rare double-bird cobalt slip decoration. Next to it stands a salt-glazed preserve jar with a bird on a stump in cobalt blue.

The top shelf displays a wide-mouth crock decorated with the vendor's name and a stoneware bottle simply carrying the name of the pottery. Below these are two lug-handled preserve crocks. On the next lower shelf is a narrow-neck canning jar with a stenciled "one" design, indicating gallon capacity. Next to it is another preserve crock in salt glaze with a stylized cobalt flower.

Ironstone

At a time when many collectibles and craft items are either very scarce or very expensive (or both), it's nice to know that some collectibles are still relatively affordable *and* easy to find. Ironstone is one of them.

This heavy, opaque white china, closely related to stoneware, was first manufactured in England, and later produced in this country in the mid-1700s. Known also as "stone china," ironstone is so named because in addition to clay, it contains iron slag.

Characterized by its durability and its ability to retain heat longer than other types of tableware, ironstone was in great demand throughout the 19th century. So popular was English ironstone in America that companies faked English marks to sell their wares.

The earliest pieces made in the 1830-1860 period are recognizable by their flowery designs accented in gold. These rather gaudy patterns were produced in extensive table services: Plates, serving dishes, and platters in every shape and size covered America's dining tables for many years.

After 1860, immense quantities of plain white ironstone were produced, many of which featured heavily embossed patterns. Some of the most successful of these were vine-leaf, grape, sheaf of wheat, lily, and garland of flowers.

Plain white ironstone with octagonal or scalloped edges also was made in large quantities. Rare examples are decorated with transfer paintings or are hand painted.

It wasn't until after 1870 that patterns became quite plain. Molds took the place of the potter's wheel, and, for the first time, potters could produce enormous quantities of ironstone at a small price. Some of the names under which ironstone was sold include White Granite, Opaque Porcelain, Flint China, and, later, Hotel Porcelain and Semi-China.

Because the field of collecting American ironstone is relatively new, it is conceivable for a collector to find complete sets that are as good as new. Large pieces such as platters, pitchers, bowls, and tureens are very desirable. Also collectible are unusual examples such as banks, molds, and footed serving pieces. Heavy embossing increases the value of any type of ironstone.

Several forms of white ironstone are attractively displayed in this mid-19th-century Pennsylvania corner cupboard, *right.* Among the less common examples are the two pudding molds on the lower shelf. The one on the left is deeply ribbed and scalloped; the other is shallower and exhibits a floral design. Also appealing are the fruit bowl on the top shelf and the footed soup tureen on the center shelf. Both feature applied handles in a classic design.

Country Collections
Woodenware

Old woodenware or "treen" is an excellent choice for the just-getting-started collector. Fine examples of these everyday wooden kitchen utensils are still easy to find, and most pieces are reasonably priced.

The most sought-after treen items are those made of burl—knotty tree growths caused by disease or insects. Though difficult to work with, burled wood was favored by craftsmen for its beautiful, unusual grain, and was used to make bowls, scoops, and smaller items. Also prized by collectors is woodenware that is painted, decorated, or signed and dated.

Woodenware is somewhat difficult to date because a few years of hard use and exposure to the elements can make new pieces look quite old. One sign of age, however, is shrinkage. Wood shrinks across the grain, producing a slightly oval shape in a round bowl or plate. Frequently, knotholes will shrink and loosen or fall out. A very old wooden object feels lighter in weight than it appears, and years of use often produce a surface that is silky smooth. Other clues of old age are the presence of wooden pegs, hand-wrought iron nails, or marks left by chisels or other hand tools.

The assortment of treen pictured in this outdoor setting represents just a small sampling of the varied shapes and forms still easily found today.

Country Collections
Painted Tinware

Painting on tin has long been recognized as an early American craft, and many forms can be found dating from 1800 to well into the 19th century.

Painted tinware (also known as "toleware") was made by pressing sheet iron through heavy rollers, then coating the thin material with tin. The flat pieces were hammered into shape, soldered, then coated with asphalt or "japan"—a black varnish used for the background. Women and young girls (often the relatives of the itinerant tradesmen who peddled the wares) applied hand-painted or stenciled decoration to the finished pieces. The results, as evidenced by the examples shown here, were charming and naïve.

Tin-painters of different regions had their own identifiable styles, but the most familiar motifs are the brightly colored designs of the Pennsylvania Dutch.

Reproductions abound in the tinware field, and examples of new painting on old tin are puzzling even to an experienced collector. Look for pieces that show signs of wear. The paint should have tiny fine age lines running through the design. Be wary of pieces that are painted inside or on the bottom. These pieces probably aren't old.

Prices of old painted tinware range from moderate to extremely expensive.

Country Collections
Quilts

Heirloom quilts and coverlets are among the most dearly loved American antiques. As highly individual expressions of needlework artistry, quilts are unsurpassed for their uniqueness of color, pattern, and elaborate designs.

In addition to their aesthetic appeal, quilts are valued by collectors for the stories they tell of the past. Many quilts that survive today were made by young girls for their marriage chests. Pieced together from frugally saved bits and scraps of fabric, the quilts were more than utilitarian bedcovers; they were expressions of a girl's or woman's stitchery expertise.

The earliest quilts were pieced, appliquéd, or put together in a combination of both methods. Pieced quilts are often intricately and artistically designed. The patterns have fascinating names describing images, events, religious motifs, and everyday occurrences.

Early appliquéd quilts were generally of floral designs, but bird and animal motifs also are seen. Swags and scalloped borders adorn elaborate examples.

Quilts vary greatly in value and desirability. Age is important, as is uniqueness of design. Condition is another consideration when buying any textile. Stay away from badly stained, worn, or deteriorating fabrics.

There are several ways to display and store quilts. Beautiful examples may be hung on the wall as artwork. With this method of display, a sleeve of muslin is hand sewn to both ends of the quilt so that a rod may be slipped through. (The two pockets allow the quilt to be rotated to prevent sagging.)

The most logical place to show off a quilt is on a bed. The one pictured *at right* is a new version of an old appliquéd tulip quilt with a lively white-on-white pattern stitched into the background fabric.

Quilts that aren't on display should be stored, rolled up or folded, in an area with good ventilation. Rolled quilts should have acid-free tissue placed between the layers. Folded quilts fare best if they're occasionally opened and refolded to prevent discoloration along the fold lines. The quilt collection pictured *above* is attractively stored and displayed in an early-19th-century painted cupboard.

Samplers

Like many other collector's items, samplers originally served a more utilitarian than decorative purpose. They were used as simple exercises to instruct young women in stitchery, numbers, spelling, and religion.

The art of making samplers was brought to this country by the colonists. The earliest examples were fashioned after English and European samplers, but American versions are generally more diverse and innovative in design. Their motifs include Bible verses, mottoes, prayers, pictures of people, houses, family genealogies, as well as the more common alphabet and numbers.

Most old samplers are made of unbleached linen, but colored linen, tiffany (a gauzelike material), and linsey-woolsey also were used. The embroidery thread used for early samplers was colored with natural dyes.

Sometimes regions or even schools had their own sampler styles. New England girls' schools, for example, are noted for pictorial or memorial motifs, and in Pennsylvania, "darning" samplers, with a wide variety of stitches, were popular.

A sampler's value is based on condition, uniqueness of design, and workmanship. Among the most prized (and expensive) early samplers are family registers (stitched histories of family names and important dates). Generally, pre-1900 samplers command the highest prices.

Boxes and Baskets

According to some experts, basketry is the oldest craft in our land. Native Indians were weaving baskets long before the first settlers arrived, and the craft has evolved since that time to produce hundreds of fascinating forms. Collectors today are fond of baskets mainly for their decorative and tactile appeal. But for hundreds of years, baskets were made, not to look at and admire, but to be used for specific, utilitarian purposes.

The term "form follows function" is an apt one for baskets; their shapes were determined by the purpose for which they were used. Baskets used for gathering crops were shaped to accommodate the crop being harvested. The same was true for baskets intended for storage or transporting purposes. This explains why they exist in so many unusual shapes and sizes.

The majority of old baskets are constructed of splint—long, flat, pliable strips of wood cut from hickory, oak, ash, and other woods. Early hand-cut splints are recognized by their thickness, their uneven quality, and marks created by tools. Newer, commercially cut splints are of uniform thickness and width.

Other materials used to make baskets include willow shoots, and numerous grasses, vines, roots, and straw. Depending on the material used, baskets may be woven, or coiled, or both.

The most famous and expensive form of basketry is the Nantucket basket. Constructed of tightly woven rattan, it is usually oval or round, and features a turned wooden bottom and a handle. Nantucket baskets still are being made today and sell for hundreds of dollars.

Attributes basket collectors look for are weave, mellow color, and form. Among serious collectors, age, condition, and rarity affect a basket's value.

Like baskets, the earliest boxes were made in a wide variety of sizes and shapes. They are as numerous and sundry in style and material as the countless uses for which they were intended. Some have hinged lids; others, sliding lids or completely separate covers. They are made of wood, bone, horn, paper, tin, silver, and pottery.

Box decoration can be plain or elaborate. Grain painting, chip carving, incised decoration, hand-painted designs, and coverings of leather, cloth, or paper are just a few of the examples a collector may come across.

Old boxes still are easily found today, but prices can vary greatly. Age, condition, rarity, form, surface, and design all help determine value. But, because boxes comprise such a vast category, most experts suggest that beginning collectors narrow their focus to a specific kind or genre of box.

Country Collections
Folk Art

Whether your taste in furnishings runs to down-home country or high-style contemporary, American folk art is an eye-catching asset in any decor.

These delightfully naïve interpretations of paintings, toys, dolls, weather vanes, and many other everyday objects were designed and made by immigrant tradesmen and craftsmen from the 17th through the 19th centuries. Although lacking in formal education and training, these imaginative folk artists employed methods and motifs that were bold, often humorous, and always unique.

Primitive paintings done on canvas, paper, or wood are one of the most popular forms of folk art. The typical painter, or "limner," was a chronicler of the times—and an artist only incidentally. Through his paintings, the traveling limner recorded social events, created straightforward schematic drawings of farms and livestock, recorded births and deaths, and immortalized the faces and personalities of his patrons.

Surviving folk art paintings boast many of the qualities associated with today's contemporary art—freshness of color, bold use of contour, and lack of perspective or depth.

Weather vanes also are regarded as valuable examples of folk art. Here again, early American craftsmen transformed their trades into art. Ornamental weather vanes were created solely to indicate wind direction when placed atop buildings. But their unique designs made them much more, and today they are prized—and often expensive—possessions.

In recent years, folk toys and dolls have become increasingly popular with collectors. Early handmade toys of wood, pottery, and cloth have an individual appeal that is universal.

Displayed on the antique pine tavern table *at left* is a small but pleasing collection of various forms of American folk art. Hanging on the wall is an early-19th-century unsigned pastel-on-paper portrait. Naïve and charming, it portrays a young man in a sensitive, aristocratic pose. To the left of the painting stands a full-bodied rooster weather vane showing an excellent surface patina that is unmistakably old. Below the weather vane is a mid-19th-century hand-carved, hand-painted Noah's Ark set, complete with many pairs of animals and Mr. and Mrs. Noah. Other items on the table include an elaborate cut-paper confirmation certificate, two homemade folk dolls in homespun clothing, and a scrimshaw storage box made of wood and whalebone.

133

Country Collections
Bears

Lovable, huggable teddy bears were first made in 1902, after Theodore Roosevelt's highly publicized hunting trip. When he refused to shoot a small bear that had strayed from its mother, his stuffed namesake—Teddy's bear—became a favorite plaything of children everywhere.

The first teddy bears were stuffed with straw and had black shoe-button eyes. Jointed arms and legs, a hump on the upper back, and a pointed long muzzle are characteristics of the early bears so avidly sought by collectors. Somewhat later bears were stuffed with kapok or wool, and had glass eyes and embroidered muzzles.

Many collectors prefer bears in as-found condition. Tattered, chewed, hug-worn bodies attest to years of child-style love and affection and add much to the bears' charm. The most valuable bears—including original teddies, bears made before World War II, and certain commemorative or anniversary bears—can fetch hundreds of dollars in antique shops. But it's possible to pay much less for bears found at house sales and flea markets.

Old teddy bears and other stuffed animals crave love and attention from their new owners. Home for this endearing menagerie is an antique splint basket. Some of the bears sport homemade clothing; all show signs of wear. The old toy train in the foreground is made of lithographed wooden blocks.

134

Country
On Display

Living With the Things You Love

For true devotees of country decorating, it's easy enough to amass a roomful—even a houseful—of collectibles, antiques, craft items, and accessories. But often, a problem arises in figuring out how to display and arrange the items to best advantage, and how to incorporate country into an existing decorating scheme. The ideas provided here and on the following pages offer many possibilities to choose from.

Though newly built, this keeping room is filled—from the quarry tile floor to the beamed ceiling—with old-fashioned comfort and welcoming warmth. Every inch of the space benefits from the presence of favorite belongings. Among the most cherished is the collection of Old Willow English china housed in an antique English hutch. Also eye-catching are the pewter plates and mugs displayed on the fireplace mantel, and the array of old utensils and baskets hanging from the ceiling.

Country on Display

Focus on Favorites

The best way to give star status to prized possessions is to place them in the context of small vignettes. In the forefront of this pleasing grouping is an old merry-go-round horse with its original paint and fittings still intact. Sharing the scene on top of an antique dough box are a grocery container from an old general store, an old pull toy, and a new handmade, hand-painted rooster. The framed primitive painting of a young child is in keeping with the theme of the collection.

The living room in this new house is a successful blend of country informality and urban flair. Given equal attention in the scheme of things are a stately Queen Anne highboy and a humble blanket chest with its original ochre grain-painted design. Perched atop the chest is a collection of folk art shore birds. Above them hangs a grain-painted candle box with its original leather hinges. A braided rug made by the homeowner underscores an antique bench.

Focus on Favorites

(continued)

What used to be a tiny closet—so shallow that coats had to be hung on pegs—is now a display cupboard for a lovely collection of Majolica. Painted deep pink and detailed with an architectural shell motif, the new cupboard greatly enhances both the collection and the room itself.

Built-in shelves, china cupboards, and niches are perfect places for displaying fragile items or all-of-one-kind country collections. Here, shelves are placed in and around a window that's been fitted with translucent glass. The glass panel filters light and effectively silhouettes a collection of redware and American Indian art. The collection continues with several items of folk art and additional examples of redware placed on a New England birch drop-leaf table.

In this living room, the addition of built-in, floor-to-ceiling shelves created showcase housing for a collector's miscellany of folk art, decoys, tobacco tins from England, and several beautiful examples of Chinese porcelain. Adjustable shelf standards promote flexibility; they can be moved up or down to accommodate collectibles of various heights. The spacious window seat, with a handy storage cupboard below, is home for the owner's favorite fowl—a large, graceful swan, hand carved by a contemporary artist. Early carved swans were used as confidence decoys to attract ducks and other aquatic birds.

Country on Display
Aim for Impact

A colorful collection of homey quilts gives this city-slick loft apartment a touch of town-and-country appeal. Adding further to the aerie ambience is a sextet of carved wooden decoys placed on a raw pine coffee table.

As a rule, collections of any kind are best appreciated, and gain maximum visual impact, when they're grouped in close proximity. Here, a cluster of large folk art houses offer a whimsical welcome to all who enter this 130-year-old country house. Inspired by tiny German village toys from the 1850s, this collection, though it looks antique, was made recently for the homeowners by local craftspersons.

144

Kitchens are ideal places for displaying old cookware and other objects from yesteryear. Here, an assortment of antique iron molds, baking pans, and trivets add country flavor to a small kitchen. What's nice, most of this decorative ironware is as useful today as it was when it was first made. Providing an atmospheric background and a good hanging surface for the collection are walls paneled with 1x12 stained pine boards. The exposed brick flue—also used as a display surface—is part of the original house.

Show Off Small Things

This gem of a lamp, with its cut-paper shade and stoneware jug base, was made by contemporary folk artist Holly Meier. Cut-paper work, also known as Scherenschnitte, is an early American folk craft. Shades like this one are painstakingly hand-cut into elaborate designs to allow light to shine through the openwork of the heavy paper. This delightful example depicts a running horse, a classic design often seen in weather vanes, cookie cutters, and punched tin work.

An enchanting collection of wooden folk toys from Germany and America fills this finely built cherry stepped-back cupboard. Placed in a dining room, the cupboard and its contents never fail to stop guests. During the 1800s, miniature toys were produced in workshops and small factories, but were hand-finished and painted so that no two were alike. For most children, these toys were reserved for play only on special occasions.

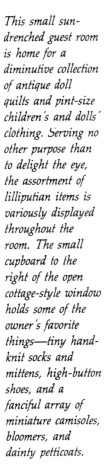

This small sun-drenched guest room is home for a diminutive collection of antique doll quilts and pint-size children's and dolls' clothing. Serving no other purpose than to delight the eye, the assortment of lilliputian items is variously displayed throughout the room. The small cupboard to the right of the open cottage-style window holds some of the owner's favorite things—tiny hand-knit socks and mittens, high-button shoes, and a fanciful array of miniature camisoles, bloomers, and dainty petticoats.

Country on Display
Accent
An Entry

An entryway or foyer is an excellent place for announcing one's love of country design. A striking example is the filled-with-flair foyer pictured here. Most arresting is the bright yellow paint treatment on the stairwell walls. This contemporary surprise element adds lively character to the carefully chosen country furnishings and accessories and serves as a decorative harbinger of what's to come in the rest of this updated Saltbox-style house.

To unify this small entry hall bisected by a stairway and three doors leading to other rooms, walls were papered in an allover thistle print punctuated by lovely painted woodwork and moldings. Country-style furnishings are simple and spare—a pine settle circa 1840, and a round table skirted to the floor in quilted cotton. The lamp is a Chinese vase that's been wired for electricity. The artwork is contemporary in nature, as is the floor. The latter was bleached, pickled, and elegantly finished in two coats of satin polyurethane.

Placed against a graceful stairway wall, this entryway vignette has the attributes of a carefully composed still life. The components of the arrangement include a Hepplewhite-style blanket chest with its original painted finish, an old braided rug, and a 1900 doll carriage complete with a doll that once belonged to the homeowner's grandmother.

Spice Up A Kitchen

A pair of carved Canadian geese adds a touch of wit to this kitchen sink window area. The homeowner, an avid collector, uses this space to rotate compositions of folk art and other just-for-fun objects. Located in a 1716 New England house, the kitchen has been newly remodeled for modern-day convenience. The custom-made raised-panel cabinets and the butcher-block counter top are new, but the low beamed ceiling, festooned with baskets, is part of the original 18th-century structure.

This sophisticated country French kitchen features a handsome 18th-century plate rack filled with a collection of old ironstone. Adding elegance to the sink and backsplash are handmade blue and white tiles. The window treatment consists of sheer cafe curtains combined with a Chamford valance. Trimmed in blue, the valance is shirred to fall in long, graceful folds.

Designed as part of a new addition to a 1777 Cape Cod house, this deep-set bowed window is a year-round source of visual pleasure for the country-loving people who live here. During the summer, family members on sink duty are greeted with a wide-angle view of the garden. In winter, the plant-filled window helps to keep gloomy weather at bay.

151

Country on Display
Highlight Your Handiwork

America's rich and varied crafts heritage is by no means a thing of the past. Today, countless fanciers of country crafts techniques are continuing tradition with their own hands—stitching, weaving, knitting, stenciling, carving, patchworking, and appliquéing. In addition to being an enjoyable, soul-satisfying pastime, crafting affords the opportunity to make beautiful, usable items for the house. Examples of present-day crafts put to decorative and practical use are the stenciled harvesttime tablecloth, dinner napkins, and chair cushions pictured here. Stenciled on plain white cotton fabric, the fruit wreath design—a symbol of "welcome to our house" in days gone by—would look equally lovely embroidered or appliquéd.

This tiny cottage-style guest room is furnished with eye-catching evidence of the owner's creative talents. The pieced-and-appliquéd quilt is an example of country crafting at its best. The finished twin-size bedcover measures 69x82 inches and consists of 20 squares of fabric measuring 9½ inches each. The quilt was assembled by alternating the appliquéd squares with the plain, cream-colored squares. Another nice example of homemade handiwork put to decorative use is the colorful crocheted toss pillow. The enamel-painted wide-plank floor echoes the blue of the quilt and contributes greatly to the special charm of the room.

Highlight Your Handiwork
(continued)

The center of interest in this cozy sitting room is a colorful handmade quilt. Hung as artwork over the fireplace mantel, the quilt sets a lighthearted mood for the room. At the fireplace hearth is a gladsome quartet of both old and newly stitched Raggedy Ann and Andy dolls. Placed on and around a child's antique wagon, the dolls serve as smile-producing accessories. An additional decorative fillip is found at the ceiling line. Here, the homeowner stenciled a stylized strawberry design to harmonize with the motifs in the quilt.

Handcrafted rugs—be they hooked, woven, braided, or needlepointed—are handsome additions to country-style settings. Colorful rugs like this braided beauty look especially attractive when placed in juxtaposition against a hardwood floor or atop any other natural surface, such as brick, tile, or slate. But even when placed upon a carpeted floor, a textured, handmade rug is a guaranteed scene enhancer.

Country
Interiors

Living Areas: Eclectic New England

The furnishings in this cozy, low-ceilinged living room represent a mixture of places and time periods. The owners, Scottie and Rob Held, are avid travelers, and rarely do they return to their 1750 Massachusetts house without a new (or old) treasure to add to their personalized place. A favorite possession is the painted 1850 chest from Switzerland. Placed between a wing chair and an old rocking chair in the "library" end of the room, the chest is a lovely example of European-style country furniture. Displayed on the chest is a Swiss doll dressed in traditional Alpine attire.

Facing the fireplace is a spool-leg Jenny Lind daybed. A family heirloom, this fine piece of Americana has a trundle that pulls out for overnight guests. The twin contemporary sofas are new, as is the coffee table. The latter was made by topping a wheel from a cider press with a thick slab of glass.

Three Moroccan nomad rugs (two on the floor and another hung on the wall) inject color and pattern into this special country setting.

Living Areas: A Converted Carriage Barn

Connoisseurs of the country life often find themselves involved in remodeling or converting old or unusual structures into very special abodes. The living room shown here is part of a 1906 carriage house/barn that once contained horse stalls. The original wood rafters and siding were retained in the renovation. The only additions are the wall of tall, view-enhancing windows, and the circular open-hearth fireplace.

Artful informality best describes the former tack room's decor. All of the seating pieces are old, but—newly re-covered in flowered chintz and textured basket-weave fabrics—they are in perfect keeping with the English atmosphere of the architecture. The tea table is a family heirloom, as is the turn-of-the-century crystal lamp. Cream-colored linen draperies were chosen to lighten the dark walls. They're banded in hunter green and tightly gathered on a painted wooden pole.

The oak refectory table in the foreground was a truly fortuitous acquisition. The story goes that an old Boston hotel was in the process of remodeling its lobby, and management felt that the old table was not fashionable enough for the new modern decor. But before the table could be sent into storage exile, the new owners happened upon it, and were told they could *have* the table for the price of carting it away.

Living Areas: A Suburban Setting

White stuccoed walls, dark-stained woodwork, and deep-set windows give this suburban house a country cottage appeal. The comfortable seating pieces—two rolled-arm sofas, a wing chair, and an old ladder-back chair—are centrally arranged around a jewel-tone Oriental rug to create an intimate conversation area. The coffee table, *above,* is an old scrubbed pine kitchen table that's been cut down to size.

A colorful combination of provincial French fabrics works together for visual warmth and interest. The small geometric prints in red, blue, and white are accented by the bolder scale of the blue-and-white plaid. At the windows, woven matchstick blinds combine with curtain panels to filter sunlight.

165

Country Interiors
Living Areas: Designed for Collections

Mary Anne and Tom Thomson's light-filtered living room contains a carefully chosen and much-loved collection that reflects their diversity of interests. In the foreground stands an antique pine tavern table with a two-board top and breadboard ends. It holds a flock of late 1800s toy sheep enclosed by a painted wooden fence from the same period.

The coffee table serving a pair of 1930s reupholstered chairs is an antique water bench, with its original red paint still intact. Other old painted pieces include the rod-back side chair, the child's ladder-back chair, and a rare half-moon pine table. Seated on the child's chair is a circa-1860 doll with a painted face and homespun clothing. In close proximity are a pair of wooden goose decoys and a stack of baskets made by Eastern woodlands Indians during the late 19th century.

The striking 19th-century hooked rug hanging over the fireplace is a variation of a log cabin design. Another hooked rug graces the highly polished hardwood floor. It provides color and pattern for the neutral scheme, and defines the cozy fireside seating area.

Living Areas: A Mostly Modern Mix

When country combines with city sophistication, the results can be arresting. Here, against a dramatic background of glazed red-orange walls and a bleached and pickled floor, a worldly amalgamation of modern art, furnishings, and accessories coexists beautifully. Country influences come from the old oak chest next to the fireplace, the wire-arm chandelier, and a 19th-century pine dining table that's been cleverly put to use as an end table for two sofas. The throw on the sofa is a modern version of an American patchwork quilt.

The wall glazing process involved painting the wall ivory, then applying a coat of clear glaze colored by artist's pigment. For texture, the glaze was combed after 24 hours.

Living Areas: An Architect's Airy Abode

This 130-year-old farmhouse is home and studio for a country-loving architect. The house—having undergone a careful renovation that tailored the space to a more contemporary life-style—still retains many of its rural antecedents.

The open-plan living room pictured here features a serendipitous mix of furnishings that are as sophisticated as they are easygoing. The 1930s-vintage rattan sofa and chairs are reminiscent of a north woods retreat, but they coexist beautifully with the more urbane teakwood tables and the elegant Oriental rug. (Note the magazine bins built into the chair arms—a distinct convenience for avid readers.)

Underscoring everything is a pickled yellow-pine floor—another flourish that makes this up-to-date hideaway special.

Country Interiors

Living Areas: Classic and Comfortable

Both of the rooms pictured here are furnished for comfort and here-to-stay homeness. *Above,* an open-hearth fireplace is the focal point around which antiques and upholstered pieces admix. The owner is a serious collector of early American pieces, as is evidenced by the 1810 shoe-foot hutch table, the antique settle to the right of the fireplace, and the 1750 Windsor chair. The handsome rush-seat ladder-back is a newly made version of a classic design.

Right: This inviting family room is a new addition to a 90-year-old house. Its construction represents a harmonious blending of old and new. Century-old pine support beams, salvaged from an old factory, were cut to form the new ceiling beams, the moldings, the fireplace mantel, and the tongue-and-groove flooring. Sliding glass doors and recessed lighting are contemporary concessions. The furnishings are an equally pleasing mix of past and present influences.

172

Country Interiors
Living Areas: Elegant and English

Decorated in the style of an English country manor, this living room features a sprightly lemon-yellow color scheme. To keep the exuberant color from overwhelming the room, large areas of white—in the painted wide-plank paneling, the shuttered windows and woodwork, the area rug, and numerous furniture pieces—provide just the right taming effect. Beautifully profiled against the bright yellow background is an eclectic collection of antique, reproduction, and contemporary furnishings.

Although the room is unquestionably elegant, many of the elements that give it character are simple and unpretentious. The slim Lawson sofa, for instance, is slipcovered in cotton sailcloth.

The focal point of the spacious room is the large oak Welsh dresser and the magnificent collection of 1748 horse prints that surround it.

A point to remember: Any bright color used as a background tends to accentuate the lines of all the furniture and accessories in the room. So, if you elect to employ a bold scheme, take care that your furnishings and other objects are worthy of emphasis.

Living Areas: Sun-Filled and Summery

The decorative air is simple and striking in this casual seaside home. Of great appeal are the two separate seating areas. One offers sofa sitters a spectacular view of the ocean; the other—an irresistibly inviting circle of wicker chairs— guarantees good conversation and fireplace warmth.

Wicker furniture has long been a staple on summer porches, but in recent years it has gained high status indoors. Most prized are old wicker pieces with their intricate, airy designs and their nostalgic, Victorian appeal. However, old wicker is quite expensive and often hard to come by. New versions of old pieces are readily available, as are more straightforward, contemporary designs. Imitation wicker—made from twisted paper or plastic—is available, too. When painted or lacquered, this ersatz wicker is sometimes difficult to distinguish from the real thing.

The delightful wicker armchairs pictured here were found at a yard sale, then revived with new cushions and several coats of white lacquer. They look particularly striking against the vermilion-splashed rug.

Dining Spaces: Echoes of Earlier Days

Looking much as it might have in the early 1830s, this nostalgia-evoking dining room functions beautifully today. The family that lives here believes in using—not just admiring—their collection of antique country furnishings and accessories. The one-drawer walnut harvest table and black-painted Hitchcock-style chairs see plenty of use at mealtimes, as do the various old dishes and bowls on the table.

In formal contrast to the primitive furnishings is the semi-antique Chinese rug. The blue of the rug is picked up in the painted trim on the doors and woodwork.

At the opposite end of the room, *above,* are an 1835 cherry corner cupboard and an original green-painted jelly cupboard, now used to store linens, candles, and serving pieces.

Country Interiors

Dining Spaces: Clean and Uncluttered

High ceilings, unadorned windows, and stark white walls offer an elegant, understated background for the mellow walnut antiques used in this spacious country house dining room.

Placed atop the beautifully bare hardwood floor, an antique Oriental rug provides an eye-pleasing island of color for the large needle-leg table and six 1700s-vintage Windsor chairs. Overhead, a graceful 16-candle chandelier, custom-crafted in New England, further enhances the period setting.

The antique hunt board, to the left of the dining table, makes a handy surface for serving after-dinner coffee and dessert. Other country furnishings include two large cupboards that are used to store and display dinnerware, silver, and serving pieces. A small-scale chest of drawers placed beneath the primitive-style portrait of the homeowner's children is used for storing table linens.

180

Dining Spaces: Midwestern Memories

Round oak tables with ornate pedestals and carved claw feet were very popular in turn-of-the-century America, and they're still sought after today. This 1890s example measures 52 inches in diameter, and is the centerpiece in Linda and Carter Knipping's simply furnished, midwestern-style dining room. Both Knippings are fanciers of all things country, and weekends usually find them at auctions and antique sales in Illinois, Missouri, and other Great Plains states. Among their acquisitions are six sturdy oak chairs (from a tavern in Ohio), and an early American walnut cupboard with its original glass windowpanes still intact. The latter is filled to capacity with a fine collection of old ironstone.

Adding a touch of whimsy to the setting is the etching over the fireplace, titled "Landscape With or Without Cow," by artist Jerry Points. Another carefree embellishment is the wooden swan gracing the tabletop. Hand-carved by Carter as a gift for his wife, the swan features a removable neck that allows it to assume two positions—at rest and alert.

Country Interiors:
Dining Spaces: Wood Mixed With White

Choice antiques, sparingly used, make definitive statements in both of these dining rooms. *Above,* what used to be a dreary kitchen/pantry in an 1893 shingle-style house now is a wonderfully informal and inviting dining area/sun-room.

New architectural amenities include side-by-side French doors, an earthy slate floor, and an eye-level fireplace that allows over-the-coals cooking. Diners at the down-home farm table are seated on benches and two rustic peeled bark chairs.

Right: Located in a city apartment, this small dining room is a visual showstopper. By placing the antique furnishings against a stark background of whitewashed walls and a bare wood floor, each piece is given the dramatic attention it deserves. The collection of country pieces includes a mix of American and English Windsor chairs, an 1850s farm table, and an equally old cushion-topped deacon's bench. The pewter sconces are reproductions.

184

Country Interiors
Dining Spaces: A Winning Combination

O ne of the nicest things about country furnishings is that they're so easy to combine. Here, provincial French melds with Americana for a fresh, unfettered look.

The focal point of the room is an antique hutch filled with a collection of green-and-white Dresden china. The same forest green color is repeated in the provincial mini-print wall covering and the wool area rug.

Sharing star status with the hutch is the circa-1860 American pine dining table surrounded by reproduction French rush-seat chairs. Topping the table is a graceful hand-carved folk art swan. The wrought-iron chandelier is an antique that has been electrified.

The cottage-style window treatment consists of white eyelet tie-back curtains dressed up with an elegant border of hand-printed French cotton. Shirred panels afford privacy at the lower portions of the windows and French doors.

Country Interiors

Dining Spaces: Old-World Charm

There's no denying that a basement is an unlikely place to find a dining room, but this one, *opposite*, is a winner precisely because it *is* located in a basement. Rough stone walls, wooden joists, and a painted concrete floor—the natural ac-

coutrements of many cellars—are what give this subterranean room the look and feel of a cozy country inn tavern. The primitive pie safe and the painted table and chairs are right in keeping with the rustic charm of the room.

Below: The look of early New England pervades this warm and welcoming dining room. Located in a renovated 1780s farmhouse, the room is aptly furnished with authentic American antiques and a variety of old-time country accessories.

Country Interiors
Keeping Rooms: Warmly Inviting

A true keeping room is the heart and hub of a home. It is the place where cooking, dining, and good conversation combine—usually in conjunction with a fireplace. And though it only has been in recent years that the keeping room has regained popularity in American homes—especially country-style homes—the concept is centuries old. Here are two present-day revivals.

Recycled heirloom furnishings and old architectural elements combine to make the keeping room *at right* inviting. Creating the kitchen/eating area involved removing an interior wall and, in the process, uncovering a long-hidden fireplace. The original brick was left exposed, and an old cherry mantel and surround was added. The tiled serving counter in the foreground divides the kitchen from the dining space.

Above: This keeping room is part of a large, open kitchen located in an 1815 Baltimore townhouse. The space always has served as a kitchen, and the fireplace, though no longer functional, was no doubt once used for cooking and heating.

Against a background of original ceiling beams, wood floor, brick walls, and pine cupboards, the room is furnished with a stylish amalgam of comfort, color, and warmth. A drop-leaf table (partially visible) provides dining space.

190

Bedrooms: Purely Pine

Free of clichés, but neverthe- less wonderfully cozy and comfortable, this bedroom makes a beautiful style state- ment with stripped pine fur- nishings. All of the pieces are 19th-century antiques, and all exhibit the kind of honest, straightforward simplicity that old-time country craftsmen are famous for.

The storybook bed, with its hand-carved headboard and di- minutive scrollwork crown, is the *pièce de résistance* of the room. It is placed on an angle between two windows to take advantage of the sylvan view outside. Warming up the bed it- self are softly inviting bed lin- ens in a dainty white-on-mauve wildflower print.

Unfinished louvered shutters at the windows and a polished bare wood floor are fitting choices for the contemporary cottagelike setting. A nubby- textured all-cotton woven area rug is another natural just right for the room.

Country Interiors

Bedrooms: Accent on English

Both of these bedrooms have an elegant demeanor typical of country manor houses. *At left,* an exquisite collection of antiques, mostly English, is used to create a wonderfully warm and comfortable setting. The black-lacquered Regency bed, upholstered in floral chintz, is topped with a crocheted French blanket cover and a rare old quilt from Maine. Another Regency piece—a *faux bois* caned-seat bench—anchors the foot of the bed. The painted tray-top table to the right of the door is Dutch, and the 18th-century needlepoint rug is English.

Above: Designed to cater to creature comforts, this spacious bedroom includes the ultimate luxury—a working fireplace. Other people-pleasing elements are an upholstered Martha Washington chair, a wing chair, and an antique pine desk for letter writing.

195

Bedrooms:
Canopied
Charm

Arched canopy beds first came into being in the late 1700s, and they've been popular furnishings items ever since. The cherry four-poster pictured *opposite* dates from 1860, and is an apt choice for this spacious room with its lofty, 12-foot-high ceiling. Adorning the bed are a colorful antique Irish chain quilt and another red and white quilt in a flower-basket design.

Below: The star attraction in this girl's bedroom is a stately 18th-century Sheraton four-poster, skirted in a sprightly green and white mini-print chintz and topped with a lacy, hand-tied canopy. An early-19th-century appliqué makes a colorful footnote for the heirloom linen bedcover.

The same country-style chintz used for the dust ruffle is repeated at the windows, and again on the old-fashioned fainting couch. The couch was a lucky find at a house sale, and now is used as a cozy spot for reading and window gazing. Other carefully selected furnishings include the continuous-arm Windsor chair in the foreground, and a bowfront Sheraton storage chest topped with a newly electrified oil lamp.

Bedrooms: Summer-House Simplicity

Country comes naturally to summer cottages and other vacation retreats; good examples are the beach-house bedrooms pictured here. *Above,* an *ad hoc* assortment of old table linens makes charming, conversation-piece dust skirts and coverlets for the twin beds in this Cape Cod guest room. Another bit of decorative improvisation: The swags hung at the head of the beds (one shown) are actually just pieces of painted wood.

Right: Awash with ambient color and light, this simply furnished seaside bedroom is a joy to look at and a snap to keep clean. The wide-plank floor, painted with yellow high-gloss deck enamel, and protected by several coats of polyurethane, is the perfect choice for beach-house comings and goings, and attendant tracked-in sand. When needed, the cotton area rug gets tossed in the wash and hung on a clothesline to dry.

Country Interiors
Bedrooms: Striking Simplicity

Farm-fresh furnishings in city surroundings is what this bedroom is all about. Marked by the absence of extraneous possessions, the room is a beautiful example of the art of understatement.

Though not all lovers of country decorating would agree, design restraint is something to aim for if you have items of beauty that deserve showing off. True, it's not always easy to pare down, but the effort is worth a try. By assiduously editing your belongings, you'll give visual top billing to the things that truly merit design attention.

Here, stark white, unadorned walls and ceiling emphasize the stately, city-style architecture while dramatizing the presence of each piece of furniture.

The four-poster bed is an antique reproduction, but the Shaker quilt rack, the blanket chest, and other wood pieces date from the 1800s. Although the swing-arm bedside lamps are contemporary, they're in perfect keeping with the simplicity of the scheme.

Bedrooms: Just Right for Relaxing

A sense of snugness and comfort pervades this woodsy bedroom retreat. The low pine-paneled ceiling and the plush wall-to-wall carpet add greatly to the cozy allure of the room, but the decorative elements are equally appealing. Chief among them is the distinctive pencil-post bed. It's a maple reproduction that's been antiqued with a deep red stain.

A true-to-tradition patterned fabric is another comfort inducer. Generously repeated on the bed, windows, and walls, the dark-color fabric is instrumental in making this room soothing and serene. To avoid monotony, the classic wing chair is upholstered in a reverse blue-and-white mini-print design.

Providing warm, glowing light apropos to the setting is a pair of antique glass oil lamps, now wired for electricity. The metal canister lamp on the desk has been similarly wired for present-day use.

Bedrooms: A Tempting Trio

What makes this room, *opposite,* so enchanting—aside from the huge windows and the Victorian bed—is the floor covering. Although it looks like an expensive needlepoint rug or an Axminster carpet, the covering, surprisingly, is wallpaper.

To create your own paper covering, first make sure your floor surface is in top condition, even if it entails laying a sub-floor of tempered hardboard. Secure the subfloor to your old flooring with drywall screws.

Then, apply the wall covering to the floor in the same manner as you'd paper a wall. Let it dry, then seal and protect the surface by applying four coats of satin-finish polyurethane. *Caution:* Test the polyurethane on your paper because it may tint the covering.

Top left: This master bedroom is located in an old midwestern gingerbread house that the owners lovingly restored themselves. It's a cheerful, homey room, filled with light and furnished with nothing-fancy heirlooms and country auction antiques.

A wedding-ring quilt from the homeowners' vast collection rests at the foot of the brass bed. Starched white eyelet pillow shams and dust ruffles complement the crocheted rose-within-a-square patterned spread. Old-time samplers, carefully protected under glass, decorate the walls.

Bottom left: The country look of this girl's bedroom comes all the way from Scandinavia. The wallpaper, a whimsical blue-on-white heart pattern, was purchased by the homeowner while on a trip to her native homeland, Sweden. The rya rug, and the multistriped fabric used as a comforter cover, also have Nordic origins.

Clear-as-a-bell colors and simple, functional furnishings are Scandinavian design precepts that are naturally compatible with the American country look. The unpretentious oak bed, chair, and desk would be just as at home in Stockholm as they are in this newly renovated New England Colonial house. The same goes for the clean-lined, white-painted shutters at the window.

205

Country Interiors

Kitchens: Combine The Past And Present

Country kitchens are not indigenous to any one period or place, nor are they bound by a particular design dictum. For some people, country conjures up images of a kitchen that's down-home, rustic, and cozily cluttered. For others, however, the term is just as likely to evoke a vision of understated European-style ambience.

Located in a 75-year-old home, this newly remodeled kitchen reflects the best of both design genres—American and European. New white-painted wooden cabinets with glass insets and crystal knobs call to mind a butler's pantry in a turn-of-the-century home. A provincial print fabric shirred on the window insets conceals the cabinet contents.

Old brick, butcher block counter tops, imported wall tiles, pine beams festooned with baskets and dried herbs, and a quarry tile floor all work together to create a warm and pleasing atmosphere. *continued*

Located just off the kitchen proper is a delightful sitting room/dining area. It, too, was included in the remodeling process. The most notable new features are the two floor-to-ceiling glass-fronted storage units. They were custom-designed to hold china, stemware, table linens, and runover gear from the kitchen.

The cabinets create a niche for a magnificent English pine hutch, which displays reproduction Calico china and a trio of antique pieces. The hutch sets the country mood for the entire room and balances the sleek, contemporary look of the adjacent cabinets.

Kitchens: An Old Room New Again

Pictured here are three views of a huge, old kitchen that's been treated to a stylish, sophisticated redo. The original room was hopelessly outdated and had little going for it except a wonderful (still working) vintage stove, *top left,* and beautiful cabinetry with glass-door cupboards, *opposite.* Using these old-fashioned features as a starting point, designer Linda Levy turned the room into an inviting provincial-style kitchen, with plenty of space for family dining, relaxing, and entertaining.

The first order of business—to cozy-up the cavernous space and brighten its depressing demeanor—involved making a number of changes, most of them cosmetic.

Immediate, eye-pleasing results were obtained by papering the walls, placing beams on the ceiling, and resurfacing the worn-out linoleum floor. The vinyl wall covering—featuring tiny white teardrops on a French blue background—has a wonderful warming effect on the room. The add-on pine beams, stained brown with a tint of mauve, succeed in visually lowering the ceiling and cozying the lofty space. White textured ceramic tiles, laid on the diagonal, take the place of the old flooring.

A fanciful "animal ring" chandelier is the focal point of the kitchen's dining area. Made of metal and painted antique white, the new chandelier not only adds great flair to the room, but does a beautiful job of illuminating the skirted table and accompanying provincial-style chairs. Another new item is the small settee to the right of the stove, *opposite bottom.* Topped with pillows in bright country prints, the settee was custom-made to fit the space.

Kitchens: Elegant Ideas

Though relatively small in size, this new kitchen is grand in style and visual appeal. Color and structural detailing, along with a nine-foot-high ceiling, create the look of an elegant European manor house.

An imported tile mural over the gas cooktop is the *pièce de résistance* of the room. Also striking is the blue granite pastry slab to the left of the built-in wall ovens, and the ceramic tile work counters.

Moldings are another distinctive feature of this kitchen. The 4½-inch crown molding is mounted above 1x6s, and the two elements are painted in gradient shades of blue to emphasize the detailing. Additional carefully fitted moldings surround the range hood, the windows, and the pass-through to the dining room.

Special storage features include the banks of drawers below counter level, and a shallow cabinet, *right,* for storing mugs and dish towels.

Also worthy of note is the hardwood floor and the ornate brass light fixtures: Both add greatly to the kitchen's classy country look.

Country Interiors
Kitchens: Focus on Americana

Antiques and collections are the decorative keynotes in this comfortable live-in kitchen. The owner, an interior designer and longtime aficionado of Americana, wanted a kitchen that would function like new but look like an old-fashioned keeping room. To accomplish this end, the original conventional kitchen was completely gutted then remodeled. From the red plaid carpet to the gingham-patterned plastic laminate counter tops, and from the patchwork wing chair to the daybed-turned-settee, this kitchen is wonderfully personal and inviting.

Custom-built cabinets feature barn board fronts, as do the dishwasher and under-the-counter cabinets. A built-in oven to the left of the fireplace is fronted with an iron door that looks antique but actually is new. The cabinets above and below the oven hold baking paraphernalia and wood for the fireplace, respectively.

The pine dining table and the two rush-seat chairs are antiques, as are all the polished copper items displayed throughout the room.

Country Interiors
Kitchens: Show Off Collectibles

A kitchen is the perfect place to put collections on display. Rustic kitchens—with their beamed ceilings, open shelves, and natural finish materials—are particularly suited to an influx of accessories.

In the kitchen *at right*, the ceiling is the show-off spot for shining copper cookware, and an assortment of decorative baskets. Other baskets are used as containers for flowering plants. The wooden swan gracing the mantel is a prized possession.

For many people, the kitchen is the heart of the home. Such is the status of the kitchen *above;* in fact, Christmas is celebrated here. Homespun cloth, cherished quilts, and a delightful flock of barnyard ornaments bring the charm of a country Christmas right into the room.

216

Kitchens: Country Contemporary

Here's proof that country and contemporary influences can beautifully coexist. Amid baskets, beams, and old pine pieces is an unquestionably modern oak table and a quartet of Marcel Breuer's Cesca chairs. Add to this the sweep of stark white tile and the effect is truly sensational. Shown *above* is a display of old matchboxes.

Country Interiors
Kitchens: Eclectic Appeal

The best of many design influences, carefully combined, can produce unique and dramatic results. In this loftlike apartment, country elements are but one part of an eclectic mix that includes contemporary and Oriental influences. The overall look is warm and woodsy on the one hand, sleek and high-style on the other.

The open, easygoing kitchen keeps good company with the adjoining sitting room and small dining area. A long work counter divides and defines the space. It consists of a slab of marble (rescued wainscoting from a now-defunct public building) resting on an oak counter from an old country store. Sitting on top are two Japanese bath buckets put to new and good use as containers for flowering amaryllis plants.

The casual sitting area features several varieties of Asian cane furniture, along with modern upholstered pieces. Surrounding the white-skirted dining table are four California "mule ear" chairs with original gut-thong seats.

Materials For a Country Kitchen

In planning a country kitchen, keep in mind that function and efficiency count every bit as much as character. No matter how charming a kitchen appears, it's not worth its salt unless it works. A well-designed kitchen of any style must incorporate a combination of sturdy materials—cabinets, counter tops, floors, and walls. All of these materials are available in a wide range of styles, but you may have to be diligent in your search to find just what you want. Here are some guidelines to help you narrow the choices.

Kitchen Cabinets

Your first decision in a major kitchen remodeling is whether to use stock or custom cabinets. The choice isn't always an easy one. The main advantage of custom-made cabinets is that they can be tailored to your precise needs; stock cabinets cannot. However, today's mass-produced cabinets are a far cry from their mundane, run-of-mill predecessors. Thanks to improved quality in both construction and finishing, many of today's ready-made cabinets look like their more expensive custom-made counterparts. Also available are prefabricated cabinet components that you can carry home from the store and assemble yourself.

The choice of finish is another important consideration. Wood cabinets have been popular for many years, and their quality varies widely. At the low end of the price spectrum, you'll find particleboard (compressed wood particles) with a photographed veneer finish. Many of these cabinets are unfinished inside; some are stained. If you're considering cabinets of this type, be sure to check the workmanship closely.

Selected hardwoods (or softwoods with hardwood veneers) are used in average- to high-price cabinets. Included in this category are oak, maple, walnut, birch, ash, cherry, pecan, and more expensive grades of pine.

In recent years, plastic laminate has become extremely popular. It's good looking, it comes in a rainbow of colors, and it's easy to maintain. Steel cabinets also are available.

Kinds of Cabinets

Kitchen cabinets are grouped into three categories: base, wall, and specialized components.

Base cabinets provide storage space as well as a work surface. Because of this dual purpose, solid construction is vital. Base cabinets are usually 24 inches deep and 34½ inches high. With the counter top, they are 36 inches high—the height of most dishwashers, trash compactors, and freestanding ranges. Widths of most base cabinets range from 12 to 48 inches.

Wall cabinets and upper cabinets vary in size, too. Heights range from 12 to 30 inches; widths vary from 12 to 48 inches. Most wall-hung cabinets are 12 to 13 inches deep. Adjustable shelves are a desirable feature because they can be arranged and rearranged to fit your changing storage needs.

Specialized cabinets go a long way toward kitchen organization, but they are costlier than standard-size cabinets. To save money, forgo specialty cabinets and make use of handy, modular shelf organizers.

Open shelving is another option particularly suited to country kitchens. You can construct your own shelving or buy it ready-made.

Counter Tops

When selecting counter tops for a country kitchen, keep in mind that some materials fare much better than others when exposed to heat, water, and sharp knives. In other words, don't be swayed by looks alone; consider function, too.

Plastic laminate is available in a rainbow variety of colors as well as a large assortment of look-alike finishes: wood grain, butcher block, leather, and others. Ready-made laminate counter tops are easy to install and are reasonably priced. You also can purchase the sheet goods and apply the laminate to a hardboard base yourself. If you do this, be sure to specify 1/16-inch-thick laminate; it is much more durable than 1/32-inch stock.

Plastic laminate should not be used as a cutting surface, or as a resting place for hot pots and pans. Once marred, it is nearly impossible to repair. Laminate is ideal around the sink because it is water resistant.

Butcher block is a real convenience for cooks who like to spread out their work when they chop and slice. If you've been confined to a tiny chopping block, you'll greatly enjoy the convenience of a spacious butcher block counter.

Ready-made butcher block counters with built-in backsplashes can be purchased by the linear foot. They are more expensive than laminate counters, but they may be worth the price in areas that frequently feel the edge of a knife. Butcher block inserts with stainless steel rims can be placed in existing counter tops at a reasonable cost.

Butcher block becomes pleasantly worn with age and use. Although not immune to stains and burn marks, butcher block can be kept in good shape with periodic light sandings and applications of warm mineral oil. End-grain maple is the best butcher block material. Be sure the piece you buy is at least 1½ inches thick.

Ceramic tile is a logical choice for counters that are in close proximity to an oven or range. Tile isn't harmed by heat and it's water resistant. Available in many sizes, shapes, colors, and patterns, ceramic tile is relatively expensive, but can add a great deal of character to a country kitchen.

Corian®, a registered trade name for simulated marble, is beautiful and much easier to work with than the real thing. Like wood, it can be cut and shaped with carbide-tip tools, making it a good choice for odd-size counters. Corian is easy to clean and resistant to heat marks. You can remove scratches and nicks from Corian with scouring powder or a fine grade of sandpaper. Corian, however, is an expensive counter-top material.

Marble work surfaces are elegant and expensive, though generally less costly than Corian. Marble is naturally cool, and quite sturdy, so it's an ideal material if you do a lot of pastry or candy making.

Polished granite is currently gaining in popularity for kitchen use. Available in a range of colors, granite is quite heavy and expensive, but is extremely durable and easy to maintain.

Flooring

The kind of flooring you choose for a country kitchen is largely a matter of personal taste. If it's an old-fashioned or rustic look you're after, consider hardwood floors, plank flooring, painted floors, quarry or ceramic tile, or brick. All of these materials will greatly contribute to an authentic country kitchen atmosphere.

If it's easy care and maintenance you're after, you'll probably be happier with resilient flooring designed to *look* like one of the above-mentioned materials.

These days, most resilient flooring is made of vinyl of one sort or another. You can choose from vinyl *tiles* or *sheet goods*, tiles being the least costly and easiest for the do-it-yourselfer to install. Both types are available with or without preapplied adhesive backing.

Sheet-goods products are available in hundreds of styles, patterns, and colors. The two kinds of sheet goods to remember are *inlaid* and *rotovinyl*. Inlaid vinyl floors are top of the line because they are solid vinyl, and the color and pattern go all the way to the backing. Rotovinyl flooring is made by a process that combines photography and printing. Once the design image is printed, a "wear layer" of clear vinyl or polyurethane goes on top. The thickness of the layer determines how long the rotovinyl floor will hold up. Most kinds of sheet flooring are sold in 6-, 9-, and 12-foot widths.

Wall Coverings

Here again, personal taste is the main consideration in choosing wall applications for a country kitchen. Paint and wallpaper are the least expensive and most practical coverings, but there are other attractive options. Barn siding (or paneling designed to look like siding) is a natural for a country look, as is brick (real or simulated). If you're partial to European or English country styling, consider ceramic tile, whitewashed textured walls, or natural-finish wood.

Country Houses

Country Houses
The Past Recycled

A dream come true for many people is owning or—better yet—building an authentic country home. It isn't necessary, of course, that the house actually be located in the countryside; the dream can become a reality even in a city or suburban setting. What does matter is that the structure exhibit strong ties to the past. Sometimes it's the style of the house, be it old or new, that calls up a country connection. Other times it's the vintage or heritage of the materials used in construction. Here and on the following pages we'll show you a variety of country home styles to consider.

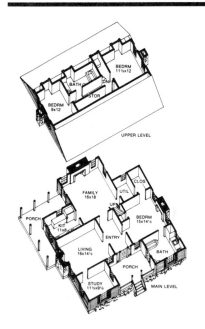

The inviting home pictured here is crafted completely of pieces from the past. Nearly all of the materials used to build the house—lumber, hand-hewn beams, bricks, glass, and hardware—were salvaged from now-demolished structures. So even though the house is new in one sense, it is more than 140 years old in another.

It took nearly 14 years for the J. Herbert West family to assemble the materials needed to construct the house. The most difficult problem was finding building materials worthy of salvaging and recycling. Much of the old lumber, for instance, was simply beyond saving. Even the salvageable items couldn't be used as found; old nails and layers of ancient paint had to be removed, and each piece of lumber had to be heat-dried before being put up. Thin panes of brittle, hand-blown glass needed to be washed by hand and chemically treated to remove decades-old accumulations of dust.

As you can see, the house that resulted from the Wests' labors of love was well worth the effort. It is a gem, both inside and out. Special features worth noting include the foundation and the three exposed chimneys. They were built with handmade Savannah gray bricks (1840) laid in Flemish bond.

continued

The exterior weatherboarding of the West house is old cypress, recut and beaded, and overlapped everywhere but under the porch roof, where it is shiplapped. The posts, porch flooring, and roof shingles also are recycled.

Materials play an important role inside the house, too. Pictured *opposite* is the Wests' favorite room—a family room/ dining area that boasts a 13-foot-high tray ceiling. The bricks in the oversize fireplace are from Lawne's Creek Parish Church (1695-1751), located in Bacons Castle, Virginia. The beautiful wide-plank floors, and the ceiling, window, and fireplace moldings also are hand-crafted relics from the past.

Like those in the rest of the house, the walls in the master bedroom, *above,* are hand-sawn, hand-planed heart pine in random widths up to 14½ inches. Because each board is unique, construction was a painstaking process of fitting. The planing marks lend a wonderful texture to the walls.

Note the door to the right of the bed: It represents the more utilitarian side of country house design. Made of unpretentious battens and planks, the door features cast-iron hinges.

Country Houses
Tradition From A Plan

Unless you're an absolute purist, there's no reason to shy away from using modern materials or an updated plan in building or remodeling a traditional country home.

The house pictured here is a reproduction of the Wareham Williams house, built in Connecticut about 1750. Although the plan captures the essence of the original New England structure, the method of construction and materials used are strictly up to date. The real Wareham Williams house was most likely drafty and subject to deteriora-

tion, but the new version is free from such flaws. Exterior walls and attic are well insulated. Zoned heating and cooling help save energy. Glass areas were reduced somewhat to lessen the escape of heat, much of which is provided by the house's seven working fireplaces.

The exterior of the house is stained pine siding. Bricks used for the foundation are new, but crafted to look like the bricks made in wooden molds. A local artisan hand-carved the broken pediment over the double entry doors, but the doors themselves are relics from the past (they were recycled from an early 1800s church).

To ensure that proportions remained authentic, much of the exterior trim work was custom made. Even the detached garage (to the left of the house) was given a special hardware treatment to visually comply with traditional New England colonial design. *continued*

Tradition
From a Plan
(continued)

What gives this house-from-a-plan such authentic appeal is the presence of small but effective architectural and decorative detailing throughout. Special touches in the dining room include shuttered sash windows with "12 over 12" glass panes. (This type of window design was quite common during colonial times because glass was in short supply and, thus, very expensive. Should a window get broken, it was far less costly to replace a single small pane than a large sheet of glass.)

Furnished simply but elegantly with a drop-leaf Queen Anne table and Chippendale chairs, the dining room has its own separate entry that leads to the garden outside. (Years ago, this room served as a funeral parlor for the preacher who lived here, and the door was made extra wide so that caskets could be carried in and out of the house without having to use the main entrance.)

Blue-painted woodwork gives the room character, as does the graceful wire-arm chandelier, and the wide-plank floor topped with an Oriental rug.

continued

As in the rest of the house, the living room, *above,* features 1x12 pine floors laid in place with square-head nails. To make the boards look older than they really are, builder Howard Atkinson devised a special treatment. He spread a light coating of sand around the floor, and then let the comings and goings of workers produce just the right amount of wear.

Here again, chair rails, ceiling beams, and wooden shutters contribute greatly to the colonial ambience of the room.

The door behind the armchair leads to the homeowners' favorite place in the house—the keeping-room-style kitchen and dining area, *opposite.* During the cold-weather months, the large, open-hearth fireplace has a magnetic attraction for all who enter the room. During the summer, it's the big bay window overlooking the backyard that draws people to gather at the old harvest table.

A Barn-Style House

Braced-frame construction is an all-but-forgotten building technique that hails from New England via Great Britain and northern Europe. Used primarily (but not entirely) in the building of barns, this special framing method was employed in the construction of the house

shown here. Authentic right down to its pegged mortise-and-tenon joints, the barn-style home is entirely handmade from New England oak that was precut then shipped to the wooded building site.

What makes braced-frame construction so special is that it resembles fine cabinetwork both inside and out. Wherever posts, beams, or braces meet, the fit is snugly mortised, dovetailed, or rabbet-lapped.

No nails are used in this type of construction. Instead, joints are secured with wooden pegs and wedges, which expand and contract from weather changes as the rest of the joint does.

Although the initial cost for building materials is relatively high in braced-frame construction, the final cost is approximately the same as that of a conventional building. This is because much of the interior framing is exposed (the framing *is* the finish), greatly reducing building time and the amount of materials needed. *continued*

237

A Barn-Style House

(continued)

As you can see, braced-frame construction offers great rewards in terms of interior drama. The central core of the house, *right,* is open all the way to the roof peak (see floor plan on the previous page). Catwalks span the spaces between the three exposed levels.

The spacious, open-plan design in no way detracts from the sense of intimacy in the main living area, *above.* Tucked under a low beamed ceiling, the area is enhanced by a book-lined wall, a fireplace, and comfortable modular seating pieces placed in a horseshoe arrangement. The natural textures of brick and wood contribute greatly to the relaxed, inviting atmosphere.

238

A Livable Log House

The oday's log houses bear little resemblance to their rustic, vacation-retreat counterparts. Far from being primitive or makeshift in appearance or amenities offered, present-day log structures are built to function as comfortable year-round homes.

Design inspiration for this log house came from a Vermont sugarhouse and a nearby 80-year-old cabin. The owner wanted a home that would combine the best qualities of each, and this is the handsome, custom-styled result.

Nestled snugly in a grove of fir trees, the home's most distinctive feature is its two-story bay. To construct the semicircular wall of vertical logs, the manufacturer had to develop an innovative system of bolts and threaded steel rods.

Surprisingly, the living room bay helps to keep the house cozy and warm during the winter months. The bay's great height aids the natural convection of warm air, allowing heat from the wood-burning fireplace to rise and enter the second-floor living space through shuttered openings. The system is highly efficient. An electric backup heater installed upstairs is used only during severely cold weather. A second heater downstairs is used occasionally to warm two back bedrooms.

The house is equally energy-efficient during the summer. Then, clerestory windows allow hot air to escape and help to pull cool air into the top-floor sleeping areas.

The interior walls of the entire house *(see following page)* are coated with clear polyurethane, so the home is virtually maintenance free. And, like all log homes, this one will never need exterior painting. *continued*

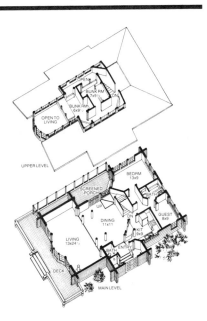

241

Log Homes: Buying and Building Tips

Log homes are so popular that more than 200 companies now manufacture them in kit form. If you are thinking of building a log home, you'll want to check the offerings of as many of these manufacturers as possible. But don't rely on photographs alone. The look of a house is important, of course, but there are other things to consider as well.

Know Your Logs

Most importantly, familiarize yourself with logs. There are many kinds available, including red cedar, white cedar, pine, spruce, and cypress; round logs, D-shaped logs, square logs; solid logs and hollow logs. They range in size from 5 to 12 inches in diameter. The various species of wood don't differ much from each other structurally. However, the diameter of a log does affect its insulating capability—the bigger the diameter, the better the insulation. The shape of a log will affect the appearance of the house. For example, a D-shaped log is round on the house exterior, but looks like paneling inside.

Of great significance is knowing how much moisture the logs contain at the time they are used to construct the house. Some companies sell green timber cut from living trees, which contain a lot of water. Several companies sell logs cut from standing-dead trees, which have had years to dry. Few sell logs that are cut green and stored until the moisture content drops to 15 percent or less. (This raises the manufacturer's overhead, and the expenses must be passed on to the log kit buyers.)

A dry log is stable; it doesn't go through any noticeable changes after it's in the wall. A green log, however, does change after it dries. Log home builders who know what they're doing can build equally sound and airtight houses of both types of logs. But green logs can cause problems if planning is inadequate or if shortcuts are taken. (A green log 8 inches in diameter can shrink by as much as ½ inch as it dries; an 8-foot wall of green logs might settle 4 to 6 inches. You can imagine what would happen if windows and doors were snugly installed before the shrinking started.)

If you're considering standing-dead timber, don't be concerned about the cause of death. Some trees are killed by fire, some die of old age, and most are killed by insects. None of these causes has a measurable effect on the ultimate strength of the wood, and bugs are rarely a problem in logs that have been dead for years. Also, most manufacturers treat their logs to prevent new infestation, and this kills any old bugs, too.

Energy and Cost Considerations

When it comes to energy-efficiency, logs are excellent insulators. Anyone who has lived in a well-built log house for any length of time will tell you that the interior stays cool in the summer and warm in the winter. A log house that has no additional insulation in its walls can be 25 to 30 percent more energy-efficient than a conventionally insulated frame house.

Cost is another consideration. If you simply order a kit and leave everything else to a contractor, you can expect to pay about as much for a log home as for a comparable frame house. You can save money by doing some of the work yourself, but few people have the technical know-how to construct a log home from scratch. Remember: The average kit contains 600 pieces, and roughly 2,000 man-hours of labor are needed to finish a kit house.

Country Houses
A Farmhouse Restoration

That hough subjected to a century of neglect and abuse, this 1870s Wisconsin farmhouse has managed to make a triumphant comeback as a simple but stately home. Credit for the structure's renovation and revival goes to Joel Wollum and Suzanne Moore-Wollum. They purchased the derelict house in 1979, then devoted the next 11 months to its complete restoration, both inside and out. The house, the barn, and the numerous outbuildings, pictured *above,* are surrounded by 120 rolling acres of verdant pasture, cropland, and woods.

A tremendous amount of work was involved in bringing the house—indeed, the entire farm—back to life. Much of the exterior had decayed from exposure to the fierce Wisconsin winters, and inside, the woodwork was black from age. Remedying these problems was no easy task. In addition, along with a new roof and a new paint job, the entire house had to be rewired and new plumbing installed.

During the renovation process, living conditions were Spartan. For many months, only one room of the six-bedroom farmhouse was habitable, and most meals had to be cooked on a fire outside.   *continued*

A Farmhouse Restoration

(continued)

Inside the farmhouse, great care was taken to select furnishings and fixtures that would accurately reflect the original character of the house. Painstaking research and an appreciation of the past allowed Joel and Suzanne to create an environment seemingly untouched by time. All improvements only serve to highlight the building's unique qualities.

The furnishings for the dining/sitting room, *top right,* are in keeping with what the original owners of the house might have used in their lifetimes. The 1880s ash dining chairs were obtained from a local courthouse, and the overstuffed club chairs are the "ultimate" in comfort from the 1930s.

Even the kitchen, *opposite,* is true to tradition: The refrigerator was custom-built to look like an old fashioned icebox, and the cabinets—with their beaded wainscoting—combine old and new. The marble counter tops originally formed a portion of the facing on a local bank building, and the multipaned windows are from an old university building.

The open door, *near right,* is one of the structure's many original architectural assets; the leaded glass window, *far right,* is a relic from the now-demolished Blatz (of beer fame) mansion in Milwaukee. *continued*

In contrast to the downstairs of the farmhouse, the upstairs takes a minimalist approach. The bedroom, *left and above right,* though not austere, is decidedly unadorned. Light filters through the simply curtained windows and reflects off the polished wood and white plaster, magnifying the feeling of space and suspending all sense of the world beyond.

Furnishings are few, but carefully chosen to create an atmosphere of peace and serenity. The bird's-eye maple bed and dresser were purchased at a local antique shop and both date from the 1830s.

Ornamental objects take on great importance in this quiet room. The three-dimensional tin weather vane has a unique claim to fame: Its twin appears in an Andrew Wyeth painting. The laminated nude seated nonchalantly in the middle of the floor was sculpted by a former student of Joel's.

Complementing the simplicity of the bedroom it adjoins, the bathroom, *above left,* is relatively free of frills. Old and new plumbing fixtures were combined in a compromise of efficiency and ambience.   *continued*

249

A Farmhouse Restoration

(continued)

Visitors to the farm, who occasionally include the over-
flow from a small country inn
nearby, have their choice from
among several of the bedrooms
in the main house, or they can
retreat to one of the two tiny
cottages located to the west of
the house. The cottage pictured
here was once a tractor shed on
a neighboring property; today,
with a new cedar shingle roof, a
front porch, a chimney, and an
ironstone fascia on the foundation, it stands proudly at the
foot of a clover-covered hill. Inside, a collection of old farm
tools reminds visitors of the
building's humble past. The bed
platform is extra high to make
room for storage underneath.

Pictured *opposite* is the interior
of the other guest cottage. This
one was built by Joel, and it
measures a tiny 16x18 feet. The
entire room, including the bed
platform, is finished with fir
wainscoting, a readily available
and commonly used material at
the time the original farmhouse
was built. The old outhouse
(visible through the doorway)
has been modernized.

Each guesthouse has its own
woodpile. The older structure is
warmed by an antique wood
stove; the new cottage has a
brick fireplace. (The main house
also is heated with wood. One
wood stove in the dining room
and a smaller one in the kitchen
keep the entire house comfortable during the winter months.)

251

A Brand-New Farmhouse

A house needn't be as old as the hills to exhibit a comfortable, country character. This gracious farmhouse is 1980s new, but its overall mien—including the tin roof and the old-fashioned porch—is straight from another era.

With the help of an interior designer, the homeowners devised a floor plan suited to their particular needs, then enlisted a general contractor to build the house to their specifications.

Because the house is located in a state where the weather often is sultry, plenty of thought was given to energy considerations. The traditional wide front porch, for instance, is not for appearance only; the deep overhang roof shields the house's interior from direct sunlight. Finely crafted exterior and interior shutters also help shut out the elements during the worst of both summer and winter months.

The floor plan is designed to encourage cross ventilation: The structure is only two rooms deep from front to back, and the openings between the common rooms are extra large to increase air flow. *continued*

A Brand-New Farmhouse

(continued)

High-quality materials and fine craftsmanship are evident throughout the interior of the house. Especially striking is the paneled fireplace wall in the living room, *below.* Made of heart pine salvaged from Virginia, the

wall, as well as the flooring, was custom milled to the home-owners' specifications. Antique paving brick defines the entry.

Details in the dining room, *opposite top,* include large mullioned windows, wide-board pine flooring, wainscot and chair rail, and crown molding.

The raised panels of the kitchen cabinets, *opposite bottom,* are made of the same Virginia heart pine that was used in the living room. Other handsome features include the beaded window and door casings, and the neatly pointed masonry work. Simple beams overhead and maple butcher block counter tops add to the old-time farm kitchen feeling.

Design Primer

As we mentioned earlier, there's no such thing—architecturally speaking—as a typical country home. However, a large number of country homes seem to fall into the category of traditional or Colonial design. For the next 12 pages we'll provide you with an illustrated overview of traditional home styles and a primer on the basic design elements most often found in these homes. We suggest that you use this guide as a handy reference should you decide to build or remodel a home in keeping with a country genre.

Cape Cod

These familiar cottages are found in almost every community in America. Much of their charming character comes from the story-and-a-half profile, capped off with a steeply sloping roof.

Unlike those of their symmetrical Colonial cousins, *below*, the exterior doors of Cape Cod cottages can be found anywhere along the facade.

Full-size shutters at the windows, as well as the close-cropped eaves, are hallmarks of the Cape Cod.

Cape Cod windows are multipaned, with the usual 9 over 9 panes. Doors have 6 panels, often with small lights across the top. Typically, clapboard siding protects the sides with exposures measuring 4 inches. But shingles also can be used. Chimneys, 2x2 feet or more, extend preferably from the roof's center.

Colonial

Colonial houses are easy to recognize because of their straightforward, unornamented design. Windows are tall and narrow and always are balanced in the facade. Typically, the windows have small panes of glass created by muntin bars (the intersecting pieces).

Entrance doors are located at the center of the house, trimmed with a simple surround. Later Colonial homes feature heavier trim and entrance details. The Colonial-style eaves line hugs the sidewalls with little overhang, and the roof is steeply pitched.

Although lower windows on Colonials have 9 panes over 12, or 12 over 12, upper windows have 9 over 9. Doors contain 6 panels. Clapboard siding with 4-inch exposures stops short of corners where it butts 6-inch-wide trim boards. Central chimneys, 2x2 feet, rise at least 2 feet above the roof ridge.

Saltbox

The Saltbox design evolved as early settlers outgrew their Colonial houses. These typically two-story houses were expanded by adding a lean-to, usually off the rear.

Generally, Saltboxes have the same formal balance as their Colonial predecessors. Entrance doors are centered in the facade and an equal number of windows flank them. Lower level windows have a matching twin above. Doors and shutterless windows are simply trimmed with plain boards. The massive chimney is centered.

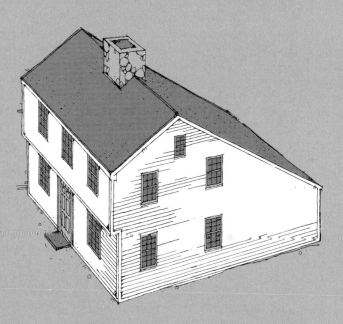

Windows are many-paned and double hung, with little trim and no shutters. Six-panel doors are common, as are solid wood-clad doors that resemble those constructed from vertical boards. Trim, here, also is understated. Siding is narrow with minimal weather exposure and terminates at boards forming corner trim.

Federal

Federal styling appears in houses built after the Revolution and begins the post-Colonial period. These houses exhibit a more stately look than their predecessors.

Here we start to see the design elements associated with Roman classicism: the use of pediments, pilasters, and columns, plus detail at the eave.

Doors are still centered, but now are flanked by columns topped with a pediment. Windows are tall and shuttered. Dormer windows project from the roof. Glass is inserted in doors rather than above them.

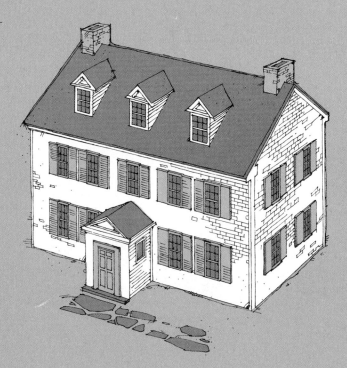

Federal-style windows feature fewer panes, usually 6 over 6 or 9 over 9. Dormer placement agrees with windows below. Six-panel doors take on a new look with panels divided in unique, imaginative ways. Federal houses are clad with brick or wood siding. Two chimneys protrude at opposite ends of the roof ridge.

Design Primer
(continued)

Plans

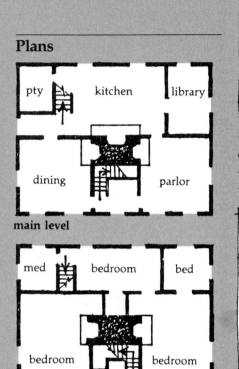

main level

upper level

True Colonial houses—those built between 1650 and 1800—would be quite unacceptable by today's living standards. They were drafty and cold in the winter, hot and often damp in the summer. Heating and cooking sources were limited to massive fireplaces. Cooling was nonexistent, as was running water, waste disposal systems, and bathrooms as we know them.

The floor plan, *above*, shows that Colonial homes were made of a collection of separate rooms, each with a specific function. Because rooms were closed in to retain precious heat, ventilation was not ideal, and traffic patterns were congested.

Shapes

Cape Cod homes are recognized by their story-and-a-half profile, lack of *door and dormer projections, and massive, centered chimney.*

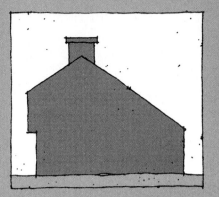

Saltbox houses feature a garrison overhang in front, with a long, sloping *rear roof line. Chimneys are large, centered, and capped with a stone slab.*

Two-story Colonials are marked by a steep roof and large central chimney. *Only a slight overhang exists, but no door or dormer projections.*

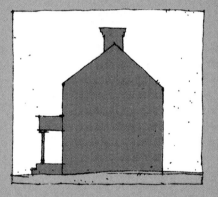

Federal houses often have a projecting porch and above-grade first floor. *Two stories and corbeled chimneys at each roof end are other features.*

Dutch Colonial styling features a gambrel roof, with a steep lower slope and shallower upper *slope. These homes often include dormers and a central chimney of brick or stone.*

Georgians are an offspring of the Federal house and use dormers to get light and air into *the upper level. The front door projects slightly, and twin chimneys top the end walls.*

258

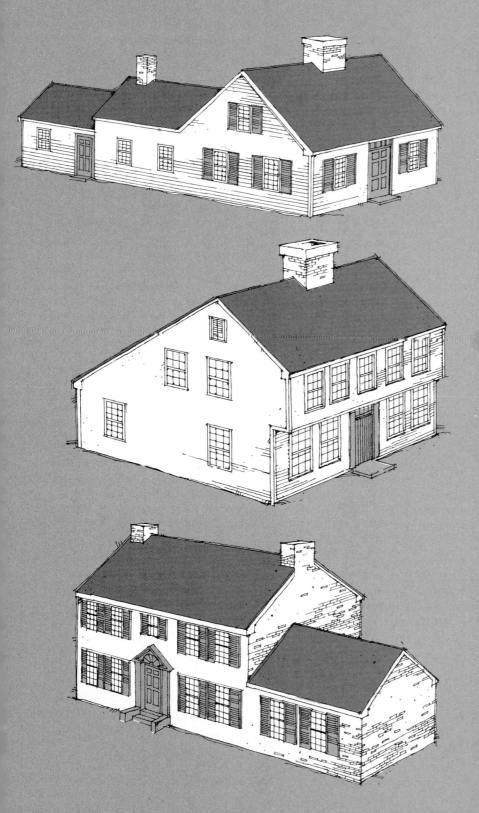

Adding On

Early American families added to their dwellings for the same reason today's homeowners do—they needed the extra space. But unlike many present-day add-ons, those of the past were carefully planned to be compatible with the original design of the house.

The Cape Cod house, *top left,* generally grew by means of an L addition—a projection added at 90 degrees to the long portion of a house. Most often, the Cape Cod L was placed to the rear of the house.

Two-story Colonial houses often grew by the addition of a lean-to off the rear. The result was the Saltbox shape, *center,* a design that has become popular in its own right. As you can see, end-wall windows are not balanced, but placed according to the division of interior space. However, the windows are uniform in size and type, and they are placed at the same head height as those on the front of the house.

The Federal house, *bottom left,* was expanded by adding a wing—usually a one-story addition of space that runs parallel to the length of the house. As indicated in the drawing, the same window placement is repeated in the addition, with two shuttered windows spaced in accordance with the other windows in the house. Today's Federal-style add-ons usually house a family room.

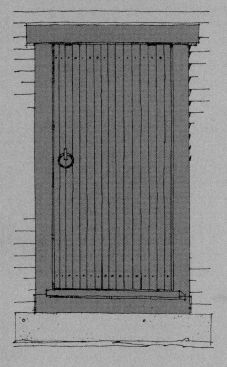

Doors

Early houses often had entry doors of vertical boards nailed to crosspieces. Trim for the door is plain board on either side, with another across the head and along the bottom. The headboard extends beyond the vertical sideboards. Note the squarehead nails that were left exposed to the weather.

Early Colonial passage doors featured the sparse trim typical of the era. Two vertical members and three horizontals frame four panels. Simple hardware was standard on interior doors. Solid, unadorned boards were used to create elegant surrounds.

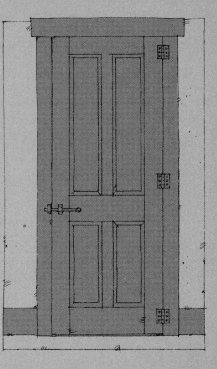

Cape Cod exterior doors were always straightforward, usually with lights. A simple surround of undecorated boards frames the door of a typical Cape Cod house. Six-panel doors are standard, and along the head doors, a row of small windows or lights often is found.

Cape Cod passage doors were the most primitive of Colonial doors. Their roughhewn boards tied together with crosspieces were used in some of the earliest houses. A simple thumb latch and pair of strap hinges are typical. Trim was purely functional, with no excess wood used.

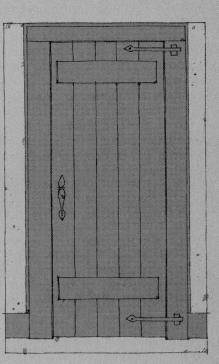

Trims

Much of the trim used on traditional houses was hand hewn. Today, machines turn out the finished product in easily assembled form—not quite as romantic a process, but much more affordable and easily reproduced in quantity.

Though the artisan quality of handcrafted molding is no longer with us, home builders today can enjoy a wide variety of materials adapted from original styles and made available at reasonable costs.

Check local lumber dealers to find trim and moldings that are in keeping with your favorite architectural style.

Columnlike supports and pediments can be constructed by a finish carpenter to create exactly the door surround you want. The fanlight, shown in the drawing above, adds authenticity.

Federal fluted columns, shown here, hold up an entablature that's topped with a dentil molding, typical of the later design motifs. This molding is a series of regularly spaced rectangular blocks.

The eaves detail is an assemblage of crown moldings applied to the fascia. The corner boards are simple 1x6 material. Any house designed in the Colonial tradition should have corner boards.

Chimneys

Chimneys are details that often are overlooked because of today's common use of prefab fireplaces. If you're building an authentic traditional home, don't settle for a prefab chimney. Instead, have a mason recreate a flue terminus in keeping with the house design.

Chimneys of traditional houses most often are made of brick, though stone also is used. Early American chimneys were massive and usually centered on the roof. Federal-style houses feature two chimneys, one on either end wall.

Here are three traditional chimneys to use as a guide.

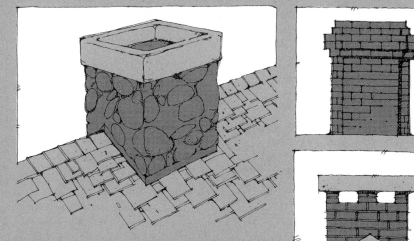

*This massive, central chimney **(above)**, rendered in stone, is a typical Colonial chimney. Make sure your chimney is large enough to give it stature and visual importance.*

*Corbeling **(above)** enhances chimneys of the later Colonial period, while stone slabs **(below)** cap Federal chimneys.*

Design Primer

(continued)

Walls

The walls in early Colonial homes did not display much ornamentation. Usually, the treatment consisted of nothing more than a coat of lime wash over plaster. Wainscoting, however, was widely used. The chair rail usually was mounted 30 to 36 inches from the floor. The wainscot system—chair rail, paneling, and baseboard—would be painted to contrast with the walls. Today, carpenters can fabricate these elements by combining standard moldings.

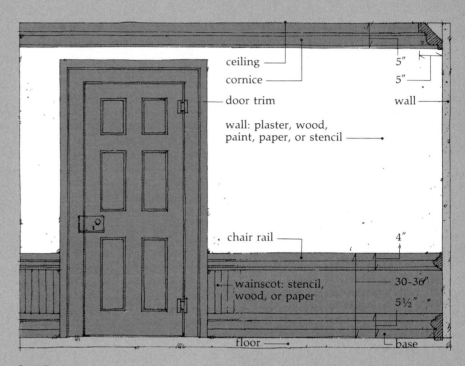

ceiling — 5"
cornice — 5"
door trim — wall
wall: plaster, wood, paint, paper, or stencil
chair rail — 4"
wainscot: stencil, wood, or paper — 30-36"
5½"
floor — base

Stenciling, a precursor of wallpaper, was (and is) a popular way to finish and decorate a wall. A pattern such as this one **(left)** *would be drawn on the wall, then painted. Numerous books are available showing traditional stencil design patterns.*

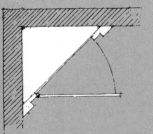

Occasionally, built-ins were added in Colonial houses and often functioned as storage units for the family's tableware. Mostly, they were corner units in the keeping room or dining room.

This corner unit **(above, left)** *takes on a classical look with rounded face boards supported by columns. Open shelves and closed cabinets provide ample storage space. The overall styling matches that of the house itself.*

The simpler wall cupboard unit **(above, right)** *is trimmed with picture-frame molding, a paneled surround, and upper glass display doors.*

Windows

Windows and doors are key details in the traditional house exterior. Windows can be flanked with shutters or left un-adorned. Earlier styles used shutters less often. Also, earlier houses featured more panes per window than later houses, though in both cases windows were typically a double-hung type. Whatever your choice, specify insulating glass.

Doors range from the simple, vertical-board type of early houses to elaborate Federal-style doors. Today, you can re-create the vertical-board door by gluing and nailing vertical boards to a solid-core door.

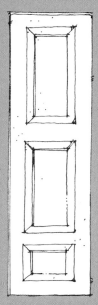

Double-hung windows were the most popular style for traditional homes. Windows were multipaned, typically nine over nine. Lower windows measured 2½ x 5½ feet; upper windows, 2½ x4 feet.

Casement windows, also popular in traditional houses, were multipaned, with muntin bars dividing the glass into small rectangles. However, in the crafting of casements, muntin bars were joined in a diamond shape.

Shutters were common in later home designs and could be either louvered or paneled. Paneled shutters usually were designed with three panels. When closed, shutters had to cover the entire window.

In traditional Colonial houses, the windows are always in balance, one over the other, with the same number of windows on either side of the door. In a facade where double windows are used at the lower level, a single unit should be located in the upper level and centered over the lower windows.

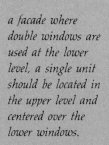

Fireplaces

Authentic, traditional fireplaces are charming to look at, but to function well, they must be designed and built with care. It is possible to have a working open-hearth fireplace like the one *top right*, but if you're planning to build a new version of an old style, be sure to hire an expert who is familiar with the kind of fireplace you have in mind.

One of the oldest American fireplace designs is the **Cape Cod** (A). This style dates from the early 1700s. Noted by its absence of extraneous trim and nonfunctional decoration, the Cape Cod is well suited to country-style homes and decors.

The **Colonial** (B) fireplace was first seen in homes built in the 1750s. A panel is set directly over the wall surface above the hearth opening, and a bit of exposed brick flanks the opening. The panel can be painted, or if the wood is fine, a stain or a clear wood finish will produce a beautiful effect.

The **Federal** (C) fireplace came into being after Colonial times. The one illustrated here is clearly more ornate than earlier fireplaces, and new features have been added—most notably, the projecting mantel. As you can see, in a Federal fireplace, the brickwork is not exposed to view.

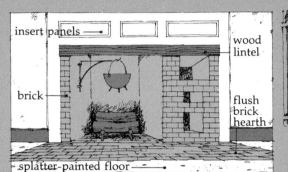

insert panels
wood lintel
brick
flush brick hearth
splatter-painted floor

Decorative hardware, like this cast-iron pot hook (left), adds country flavor to an open-hearth fireplace.

A

Brick used in Cape Cod fireplaces is of the common variety, and left in its natural color. Rugged, roughhewn boards, set flush with the brick, are natural, too.

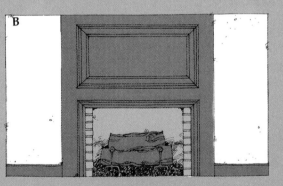

B

Trim on Colonial fireplaces was used to cover brickwork, creating a more refined appearance. Picture-frame molding outlines the fireplace opening, and the hearth is flush with the floor.

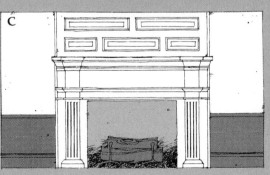

C

Five recessed panels were used over the mantel in this symmetrical design. A pair of fluted columns terminates in a shallow mantel. The color of the fireplace matches the walls.

Lighting

Earliest lighting for Colonial homes consisted of oil-burning lamps, candle lamps, and the "Betty" lamp, a grease-filled dish with a wick.

Another form of light fixture was a viselike clamp that held a lump of pine tar, or pitch. Its light was dim and the odor it produced was unpleasant.

Although it wouldn't be practical to try to light a present-day home with early lighting fixtures, old candle lamps and other rustic fixtures are great for decorative use. The lamps and fixtures shown here could easily be wired and fitted with electric candle bulbs.

The pierced-tin lamp is one of the oldest designs. It was fashioned to hung from a hook and provide perforated light in dark passageways.

The ship's lantern is a later version of the pierced-tin lamp. It, too, included a ring for hanging or carrying by hand.

The tin chandelier is another old fixture. It consists of candle holders with reflectors projecting from the core. Electric versions are popular today.

flush brick hearth

random-width flooring

The Keeping Room

The keeping room of the Colonial house was the activity center for the family. Here, food preparation, cooking, spinning, and sewing took place. The space usually was the largest room in the house, and contained a massive fireplace, which heated the area and served as the range and oven.

Floors in the room—as well as floors elsewhere in the house—were random-width boards of oak or pine. The hearth usually was brick or stone, and always was flush with the floor.

Doors were three- or six-paneled with a simple surround and a single board cap.

Ceilings most often were limed or painted rough plaster. Beams were left exposed when they served as joists for the floor above.

265

Stairs

Probably the most easy-to-duplicate element of Colonial houses is the stairway. Today, manufacturers still produce stair parts that look identical to the originals.

As did other interior elements of early houses, stair treatments started out simple and gradually became more detailed. Stairs in a Cape Cod consisted of a simple rail and vertical balusters. A lathed newel post was the only decoration. Toward the end of the Colonial era, designs became more ornate.

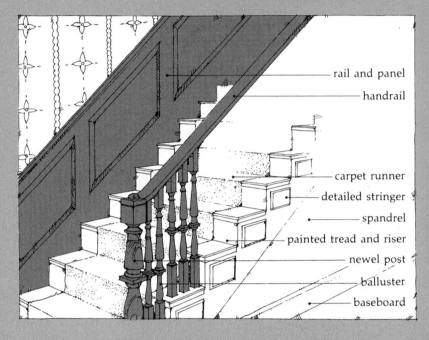

rail and panel
handrail
carpet runner
detailed stringer
spandrel
painted tread and riser
newel post
balluster
baseboard

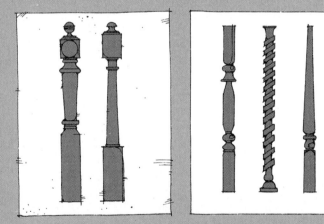

Cape Cod

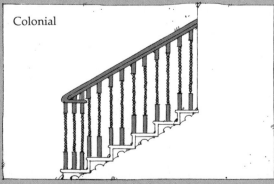

Colonial

The newel posts **(above)** *show the difference between the Federal (left) and Colonial (right) styles. Baluster design shows a trend toward decoration as the 1700s progressed.*

Shown **(above, center),** *from left to right, are the Colonial, turned, and Newport styles. Similar newel posts and balusters can be bought today.*

The Cape Cod stairway **(above,**

right) *is an early design. The turned newel post contrasts with the simple square balusters. The Colonial stairway* **(right)** *features painted treads and risers and intricate parts.*

Hardware

Security was not the hallmark of Colonial homes, but as wealth increased, so did the quality of locks and latches. Don't compromise security, however, in your quest for authenticity. Exterior doors should have a modern-day backup dead bolt in order to be effective.

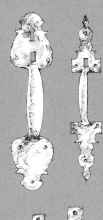

Back latches **(left and below)** were used for passage doors. The latch was mounted on one side of the door only, and thrown open when the adjoining room was being used. Similar hardware can sometimes be found on gates and outbuilding doors.

Thumb latches **(right)** were typical on passage doors. The Suffolk latch, shown here in three pieces, would have a thumb plate on one side and a string pull on the back.

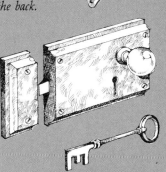

Box locks **(below, left)** were a later invention. A set would be mounted on each side of the door, with the strike plate mounted on one side of the jamb. Wrought iron was used for much hardware; brass was less common. It was possible to buy either a left- or right-hand box lock.

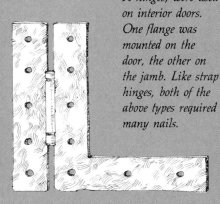

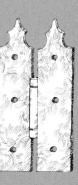

H hinges **(left)** were used on everything from passage doors to small cabinet doors. Although wrought iron was the most popular material, brass was favored for showpieces.

H-L hinges **(below, left)** like H hinges, were used on interior doors. One flange was mounted on the door, the other on the jamb. Like strap hinges, both of the above types required many nails.

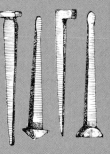

Nails and wooden pegs were the usual means of fastening materials. The four nails shown above are examples of the many types used throughout the Colonial period. Precise dating of nails is difficult. Today, you can buy standard nails with reproduction heads or nailheads with tack points.

Strap hinges **(above, left)** were used in heavy applications, such as doors and gates. Because of the load they had to support, such hinges required many nails.

Smaller strap hinges **(above, center)** were used on interior doors. An L-shape pivot was hammered into the door frame at top and bottom with door-mounted leaves hung on the pivots.

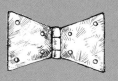

T hinges **(above, lower center)** look similar to those used today.

Early hinges, such as the wrought-iron butterfly hinge, **(left)** came in several sizes; small ones often were used on cabinets.

Researching The Roots of Your Home

Researching and compiling a history of your home, particularly if it dates back 40 years or more, can be a fascinating experience. The house need not be an architectural landmark, nor must its former owners have been famous to make the endeavor worthwhile.

Curiosity is what leads most people to research the roots of their homes. Even the most modest structure may reveal an intriguing history. By doing some digging, you can uncover facts about the house itself, glean information about the neighborhood, or learn more about the home's previous owners. From a practical standpoint, researching the history of a house can turn up facts about its structure, its wiring and plumbing specifications, and background on previous remodeling efforts. This information can come in handy should you decide to renovate, restore, or remodel your home.

Where to Look

The best place to begin your research is at the county or local assessor's office. However, not all governments are organized in the same way, so you may find your trail leading to other agencies. Most of the information you'll need is available to the public.

You'll find a wealth of information in the assessor's office, including the original cost and ownership of the land and building, its architect and builder, zoning at the time the house was built, each subsequent owner and price paid, and lists of original materials and specifications. You also may find a copy of the original plans and even a photograph of the house at the time it was first assessed. If you're remodeling, your architect or builder (if you engage one) will find photos and original plans helpful. For a small fee, you usually can obtain copies of the records you want.

In some locales, land ownership records go back to pre-statehood times. If you live in the East, for example, you may find records dating to the Colonial era even though your house was built in this century and is the second or third structure to occupy the site. These records usually are arranged by block or geographic section. Check files for houses around you to get an idea of how the neighborhood was developed.

People from the Past

To learn more about the people who used to live in your house, check old copies of city directories. They usually list the owners' names, their occupations and employers, and, sometimes, the number of children in the household. Directories also have listings by house number and street so you can determine who lived nearby and draw conclusions about the early makeup of your neighborhood.

Census files also are good research sources, as are the local history departments of public libraries. Newspaper "morgues," photo archives, and local historical societies are other likely places to obtain information about your house and the surrounding neighborhood.

Once you've gathered all the material, you can put it to use in any number of ways. One idea is to type up a simple history for your own personal enjoyment and enclose it in a loose-leaf album. If you want a more elaborate version, have it printed and bound in book form. Another idea is to work the basic facts into a plaque or a scroll, then display your home's history on the wall.

The Realities Of Restoring A Vintage House

If weekends find you scouring the countryside for the perfect vintage house, you've no doubt been bitten by the bug to buy. However, before you make a down payment, you need to consider certain realities. For starters, keep in mind that restoring or renovating an old house is a big job that requires a great deal of time and money. Remember, too, that the best bargains—those that real estate agents refer to as "handyman specials"—often are in dire need of structural repair, and may be too far gone to be saved. The following information will give you an idea of what's involved in buying and rehabilitating an old house, and will help you decide whether you're suited for such a major undertaking.

Your first order of business is to decide whether the house you're interested in is really worth saving. To get a good sense of the house's general condition, inspect the items you'd check on any house, paying particular attention to structural defects, plumbing, and electrical problems.

In making your investigation, you might want to use a checklist specially designed for vintage houses. *The Old-House Journal* offers one. (The address is 69A Seventh Ave., Brooklyn, NY 11217.) You'd be wise, too, to invest $100 to $200 for a professional building inspection. Ask someone with renovation experience to point you in the right direction, or look in the Yellow Pages under "Building Inspector Service."

Once the inspection is complete, you should receive a written report that includes estimated costs of each recommended repair. This report will help you in deciding whether to buy the house. The house may, in fact, be too far gone for your resources. Although anything can be fixed, are you willing and able to pay the price?

Will You Restore Or Renovate?

Of the two processes—restoration and renovation—the former is by far the more costly and time-consuming. Restoration involves returning a vintage home to its original condition, adhering faithfully to the tiniest details. Renovation, on the other hand, allows more flexibility. Although you still retain many of the period details, practical matters (such as the installation of triple-glazed windows) take precedence over purism.

Research: The Key To Success

In order to begin restorative work, you'll need to know what the house looked like when it was originally built, and how it changed over the years. Check your public library for old books that might carry photos and plans of your house (or houses similar to yours). Ask old-timers in the community if they can recall details of the rooms. Check old city directories for the names of previous owners who might have helpful information to share. Look up old deeds and abstracts in search of additional tips that might shed light on the home's earlier life.

Advice from the Pros

An increasing number of architects are becoming involved in restoring and renovating old homes. An architect whose first love is retaining lovely old structures can be one of your most enthusiastic and valuable resources. To find a restoration architect, check with architectural associations, talk with nearby historical and preservation groups, and with others who've rehabilitated old homes.

If you decide to retain an expert, look for someone who is familiar with the building details of the older homes in your area, has worked with the subcontractors most qualified to handle vintage restorations, and can supply sources of appropriate salvage materials.

Interior Details

The woodwork adorning a period home is one of its most valuable assets. And even if the beautiful moldings have been covered with a dozen coats of paint or abused by vandals, plan to restore them completely. If you can't find replacement trim in a salvage shop, have a craftsperson make duplicates from the originals.

Hardware, too, is a replaceable item; you either can buy salvaged pieces dating back to the same period, or send a sample to a firm that makes accurate reproductions.

The old wood floors common to country homes are another personality item well worth saving, even though they may need to be patched and refinished. Sagging or sloping floors are not uncommon in older homes, but unless the slope is extreme or dangerous, a leveling job is probably not worth the effort or expense.

And, finally, if your home is blessed with such special touches as ornate plasterwork, do everything possible to preserve these details. If they're beyond repair, replace them with today's replicas so you can retain the charm that makes vintage homes so appealing.

Finding Vintage Supplies

Interpretive restoration is a balance of authentic and repro-

duced supplies. You can hunt for authentic supplies at auctions or scrounge for them where houses or old buildings are being demolished. Notices of auctions and razings often are listed in the newsletters of local historical associations. For information beyond your own local area, check *Preservation News,* the newsletter of the National Trust for Historic Preservation, which has pictures and data about buildings being torn down. The NTHP also publishes a magazine, *Historic Preservation.* (For information, write to the National Trust for Historic Preservation, 748 Jackson Place NW, Washington, DC 20006.)

Reproductions of everything from cast-iron tracery to whimsical wooden gingerbread are available today. *The Old-House Journal* publishes an annual catalog of dealers conveniently listed according to supplies they furnish. (See opposite page for the address.)

Exterior Repairs

The most beautiful interior renovation is worthless unless the exterior is in good repair as well. Heed the time-proven advice that the roof and foundation are your primary concerns; everything else is secondary.

Foundation: Most century-old foundations, though basically sound, need at least some repairs. A few need to be replaced completely, and your restoration architect can help you find someone experienced with stonework. (Or you may opt for poured concrete—another decision based on how committed you are to authenticity.)

Roof: Whether your roof is slate, tile, tin, wood-shingle, or

clapboard, you usually can replace or repair it with identical materials. And you may decide that the low cost of asphalt shingles makes them an acceptable substitute, again depending on your leaning toward purism.

Siding: Carefully check the structure's siding for signs of water leaks and damage. Masonry homes, usually either brick or native stone, probably have deteriorated mortar. And the walls themselves may have bowed or sagged because of settlement. Fortunately, experienced masons can repair the damage. Wood shingles or horizontal siding is easier to fix. Even if you have to replace a bad section, a good millwork firm can produce excellent replicas of siding patterns.

Mechanical Systems

Only the true purist will be content with an old-fashioned heating system such as a fireplace. However, if the home is equipped with an old-type wood stove, you may be able to live comfortably, particularly if you add a few electric baseboard units as backup.

Because the cost of heating and cooling a vintage country home can be almost prohibitive, plan your energy strategy long before you begin the actual work. Insulation is your main defense. Plan to install it in the attic, crawl spaces, and walls. You can fill the wall cavities either by blowing loose insulation through holes drilled in the walls, or by installing batts or rigid foam when the cavities are exposed for other restoration work. Try hard to minimize harm to the period details you want to protect the most.

Country Gardens

Country Gardens
Country Airs

Just as a country-style house can be located anywhere, so can a country garden. Certainly a rural setting offers the best possibility for a penultimate flower garden, herb garden, or vegetable patch, but city and suburban locales are not without promise. With thoughtful, imaginative planning, even the smallest plot of land can be magically transformed to exhibit country airs. The essence of a country garden, after all, is its unpretentious mien. Size is secondary to charm and ambience. Wherever you live, the idea is to strive for a garden, large or small, that will delight your senses and gladden your spirits.

Natural, carefree, and undemanding best describes the garden pictured here. Daylilies and liatris team up to provide an inviting, storybook introduction to the rustic, barn-sided house. The best thing about these flowers—in addition to their insouciant beauty—is that they're practically maintenance free. Weeks before blooming, the daylily forms a lush ground cover. Later, because the foliage becomes so dense, very little weeding is needed. Plant daylilies and liatris in the sun or in partial shade and they will provide spectacular bloom from June to September.

Country Gardens
Wildlife Gardens

With a little careful planning, a country garden can become an oasis for a host of colorful birds, butterflies, and small animals. That's why, when you plan your garden, you should keep wildlife in mind.

Always give planting preferences to seed-, nectar-, and fruit-producing species favored by wildlife. Blackberry, raspberry, honeysuckle, viburnum, nannyberry, gooseberry, highbush cranberry, pyracantha, currant, bittersweet, and dogwood are just a few of the many fruit-bearing shrubs and vines that are especially attractive to wildlife. Annual and perennial flowers such as bee balm, sunflower, poppy, aster, daisy, marigold, cosmos, and tithonia will entice both birds and butterflies into your yard. Tree species that are favorites of wildlife include beech, box elder, spruce, wild cherry, apple, mountain ash, mulberry, hackberry, and oak.

Fragrant spires of lavender (above) attract bees and other important insect pollinators. Plus, you can save the spent blooms for potpourris.

Although lavender is a perennial, it does require some winter protection in northern gardens. After hard frost, cover the plants with evergreen boughs, leaves, or straw.

If you want to entice butterflies to your yard, plant annual flowers like tithonia, zinnia, and marigold. Some flowering shrubs that will bring butterflies to your garden include buddleia, lilac, and viburnum.

Bird feeders, birdbaths, and birdhouses (above) located strategically throughout the garden are important wildlife attractions. When you place these receptacles in the garden, remember to locate them near shrubs or tall plants; birds are more likely to use them if they know an escape route is nearby.

279

*Yarrow, which is sometimes classified as a perennial and sometimes classified as an herb, is an eye-catching addition to any wildlife garden **(top)**. Other herbs that are attractive to wildlife are mint, chamomile, borage, chives, sweet basil, lemon verbena, tansy, caraway, and comfrey.*

*If you want an old-fashioned touch in your garden, why not add a weathered rain barrel **(above)** beneath an eave spout? You can use the collected water on tender indoor plants like African violets.*

Water, in any type of container, will always draw wildlife visitors. The cement pool (left) becomes the centerpiece of the garden, creating a refreshing retreat for birds and people.

You can build a small cement pool like this one, or you can purchase a commercial fiber glass pool and sink it into the ground. Then, add a colorful assortment of aquatic plants.

Evening primrose (above) is a hardy perennial requiring little care. It offers spun-gold blooms in late June. Two popular evening primrose varieties include Ozark Sundrop and Highlight. Plant both varieties 12 inches apart in either spring or fall.

281

Country Gardens
Tulips

Fringed tulips **(top)** *grow about 22 inches tall and bloom in mid- to late May.*

Darwin hybrid tulips like Vivex **(above)** *are available in an almost unlimited assortment of colors. They bloom from late April to early May.*

Unlike other tulips that produce

only one flower per stem, the multiflowered types can produce as many as six flowers at one time. Orange Bouquet **(top)** *is one of the best multiflowered tulips.*

Oriental Splendour **(above)** *is an unbeatable bicolored species tulip that grows ten inches high and blooms in April.*

Tulips originated in Turkey, and when they were introduced in Europe 400 years ago, they triggered a continental craze. The demand for imported tulips so exceeded the supply that some of the rarer varieties sold for thousands of dollars. The resulting economic bubble was known as "tulipomania."

Eventually tulip fever abated, but the tulip has remained one of the most popular of all garden flowers.

Tulips generally are divided into 15 classes, which vary in appearance and season of bloom. The early bloomers include single early and double early. Some of the mid-season bloomers are mendel, triumph, and darwin hybrid. Late- or May-flowering tulips include darwin, lily-flowered, cottage, rembrandt, parrot, and double late. And, for extra-early flowers, plant tulips such as kaufmanniana, fosterana, greigi, and other species.

You can show off tulips alone, or use them to brighten a

perennial or shrub border. But for a continuous show of color in an all-tulip bed, be sure to plant a combination of early-, mid-, and late-flowering varieties. Use the early-blooming varieties in front of the mid- and late-season tulips and save the shorter species tulips for the border edge or rock garden.

For best results, tulips need a period of cold and darkness to bloom. In northern climates, plant tulips in the fall before the ground freezes hard. In southern locations where winter temperatures do not regularly drop below freezing, tulips are best treated as annuals. You can buy prechilled bulbs and set them out in the spring, or you can buy bulbs eight to ten weeks before planting time and chill them in your refrigerator.

Tulips grow well in almost any type of soil, but be sure the planting site is well drained. Standing water will rot the bulbs. Tulips also prefer a sunny location, but a spot that receives a little late-afternoon shade is just as good.

Country Gardens

Daffodils, Crocuses, and Hyacinths

No country garden is complete without a sunny collection of spirit-lifting daffodils. Like tulips, these hardy bloomers should be planted in the fall before the soil freezes. And with a little careful planning, you can choose an assortment of varieties that will bloom from late March to mid-May.

Most daffodils live for many years and increase in quantity and beauty each spring. Planting depths are important, as is conditioning the soil deep beneath the bulbs. Bulbs of standard-size daffodils must be planted eight inches deep (measured from the rounded shoulder of the bulb). Miniature varieties should be planted three to four inches deep.

Daffodils look best when they're planted in groups of six or more bulbs. The best way to plant these groupings is to excavate the planting area to a depth of four or five inches and turn the soil in the bottom of the hole a full spade's depth. If the soil is heavy, add sand and vermiculite or perlite to loosen it. Then space the bulbs over the surface of the soil and dig individual holes.

In the excavated areas, you'll need to dig holes only three or four inches deep to set the bulbs at their proper level. When the bulbs are in place, fill the hole until it is level with the surrounding soil. Water well at planting time and every week or so until winter arrives.

Some daffodil varieties are able to compete with low grass and may be planted here and there in an unorganized way to look as though they are growing wild in the lawn. This process, called naturalizing, is easy to accomplish. Simply take a handful of bulbs and toss them gently in an area where flowers are desired. Then, plant the bulbs where they land. For best effect, however, the bulbs should not be spaced too far apart.

After the flowers fade in the spring, the foliage must be left intact to build up the strength of the bulbs for next year's blooms. This can be a problem in flower beds, because the foliage doesn't ripen and die until late May or June. To get it out of the way of other plants, you can gather handfuls of the long slender leaves, bend them, and secure them into a topknot with rubber bands. Or, if you want to be fancy, braid the leaves as you would hair.

The nice, plump bulbs you buy are all ready for the first year's flowering and do not need plant food to produce blooms. To help the foliage fatten the bulbs for subsequent years' blossoms, scatter bulb food around the plants after the flowers fade.

284

Although they're not as popular as tulips and daffodils, deliciously fragrant hyacinths, *right,* offer the country gardener a choice of bright primary colors, not available with daffodils or tulips. Their stately, almost formal, flower heads are perfect for front-of-the-border locations where the hyacinths' color and fragrance can best be enjoyed.

Always be sure to pack as many bulbs as possible into your hyacinth border. Because of their upright growth habit, hyacinths don't wave around as much as long-stem flowers, and a loose planting can look sparse and spotty. Like other hardy bulbs, hyacinths are best planted in the fall. Plant the bulbs eight inches deep and be sure the garden soil is well drained; hyacinths are particularly sensitive to wet spots. Hyacinths grow well in partial shade, but you'll get more perfect blooms in a sunny spot that's protected from high winds.

As with other bulb plants, hyacinth foliage must be left for a month or so after bloom; the foliage helps produce food for the next season. Unfortunately, the hyacinth is less hardy than other bulbs and must be well protected in winter. It fails to produce vigorous blooms after about three years, and many gardeners find that yearly replacement is the only way to be sure they'll have flowers the following spring.

The grape hyacinth, *Muscari sp., middle right,* is not a true hyacinth, but seen from a distance it does resemble its taller cousin. These hardy little bulbs grow only eight inches tall and produce quantities of blue, violet, or white flowers. The plants spread rapidly.

In early spring, when most other garden flowers are still dormant, the crocus, *bottom left,* bursts into flower. These hardy, pint-size bloomers will grow in almost any soil and they can be left undisturbed for years, multiplying steadily, forming dense mats of color. The crystal-bright flowers come in an assortment of colors—yellow, blue, purple, lavender, and white are the most common, but striped and splotched varieties also are available.

Plant crocus bulbs approximately four inches deep and close together—only a couple of inches apart. Small clumps of bulbs are ideal when scattered under deciduous trees and shrubs and along the border edge or garden path. They also make great rock garden plants. If you like, you can naturalize your crocus in the lawn as you would daffodils. Just be sure you don't plant them where their foliage will be accidentally clipped by the lawn mower.

Because crocuses spread so rapidly, it's wise to dig, separate, and replant them every three or four years; if the plants are too thick and crowded, they will not bloom.

285

Country Gardens
Bulb How-To

The key to a successful bulb garden is good soil preparation. Your bulb bed should be well drained and rich in organic matter. Lack of sufficient drainage results in poor root growth and development of bulb rot.

Take time to improve the drainage of soil high in clay. Add sand, peat, or vermiculite to a depth of 12 inches (or a full-spade depth). If soil is too sandy, work in rich peat moss or compost.

The actual depth for planting bulbs varies according to the variety and the soil—deeper in light, sandy soil, but shallower in heavy clay. If the soil is well drained, try planting tulips ten inches deep, rather than the usual eight. An added benefit: After the foliage dies, you can plant annual flowers right over the tulips.

To plant a clump of bulbs, dig a hole nine to 12 inches deep, and replace loose soil until the depth is correct for your

bulbs (see bulb chart *opposite*). Mix in a little bone meal or bulb fertilizer; most bulbs do not require feeding their first season, but the fertilizer does improve flowering. Then, set the bulbs point up in the hole. Press them gently into the soil and cover until the hole is level with the surrounding garden.

The single most effective planting technique is to mass each bulb for maximum visual impact. Instead of lining up thin rows of bulbs like a military review, crowd favorite varieties into large blocks of brilliance.

For most hardy bulbs, the perfect planting site is an area naturally covered by light shade during the warmest part of the day. When this is provided, blooms will last longer and retain a deep color.

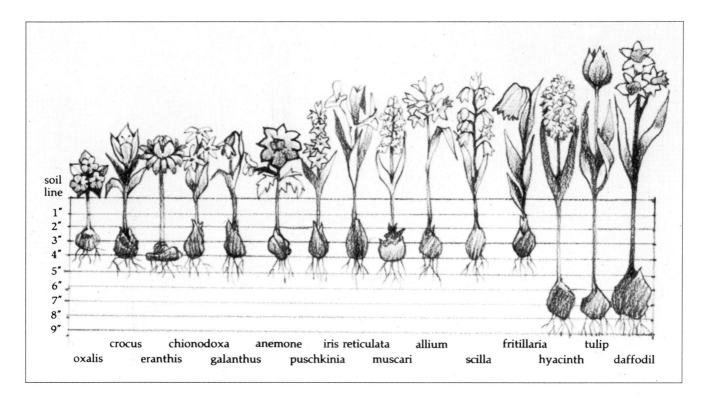

soil line
1"
2"
3"
4"
5"
6"
7"
8"
9"

crocus   chionodoxa   anemone   iris reticulata   allium   fritillaria   tulip

oxalis   eranthis   galanthus   puschkinia   muscari   scilla   hyacinth   daffodil

Afternoon shade helps prolong the life of the flowers and keeps the plants cooler. One ideal location is under deciduous trees. Here, spring-blooming daffodils, crocuses, hyacinths, and tulips can flower and develop before the trees' leaves mature. By the time the trees have a canopy of leaves, the bulbs already will be on the decline.

Unfortunately, large tree roots do compete with the bulb roots for food and water. To make sure bulbs develop well in late spring, keep them moist. They often cannot benefit from light rains or dews because the trees' roots are so competitive.

Bulbs in a south-facing bed will flower earlier in the season than those in a north-facing garden. Also, a bed sheltered by a house foundation, where soil tends to be warmer, is likely to flower earlier than one set farther away.

In the deep South and other areas that escape freezing weather, it's best to give bulbs an artificial winter. In these warm climates, the bulbs must be dug and refrigerated each year. Leave the bulbs in place until the foliage has completely ripened. Then, dig up the bulbs and store them in a dry, dark place for the summer. To precool the bulbs, place them in the bottom of your refrigerator at 40 to 50 degrees Fahrenheit for six to 12 weeks. Or purchase new bulbs that already have been precooled.

If your flower bulbs will be dug up and discarded after one season of bloom, they may be planted in areas not normally suited for perennial treatment. They even may be planted in heavily shaded areas; extensive soil preparation is not necessary.

Field mice, chipmunks, and squirrels often are a menace to newly planted bulb beds. To keep these animals from dining on your bulbs, don't set any plants next to garden walls or house foundations where the animals make runs. And before planting in the fall, clean beds of all garden waste that could make ideal nests for mice.

The only sure way to protect newly planted bulbs against four-footed pests is to place the bulbs in baskets fashioned from hardware cloth. Sink the baskets into the soil, their tops left open. These wire baskets also protect the bulbs from underground marauders such as moles and gophers.

If animal pests continue to plague your garden, you may have to trap and relocate them with a humane live trap.

287

Country Gardens
Herbs

For centuries, herbs have captivated people with their sweet fragrances, delicate foliage, and pungent flavors. The ancient Greeks and Romans worshiped herbs along with their gods. During the Middle Ages, herbs were given a place of honor in royal gardens, and landowners competed for the most intricate herbal garden designs.

In the more humble medieval cottage gardens, herbs were grown more for utility than aesthetic value. Flavorful culinary herbs were added to meat to conceal spoilage, and aromatic herbs were scattered on floors to disguise unpleasant odors.

Because they've never been subjected to extensive breeding programs, the herbs we know today are the same ones the Greeks and Romans admired. What has changed is our beliefs about herbs.

At one time, herbs were ascribed magical and godlike powers. Dill, for example, was believed to ward off witches. The slow-germinating seeds of parsley were said to be possessed by the devil. And immortality was accredited to tansy. Today, however, aside from their occasional medicinal use, herbs are loved primarily for the enchantment they lend to gardens and food recipes.

Herbs

(continued)

Although herbs will grow almost anywhere, they fare poorly in heavy, wet soils. Test your soil to see if it drains well by giving it a good soaking with a hose. If the soil fails to absorb the water within two hours, you'll need to improve it.

To facilitate drainage, spade the soil to a depth of 12 inches, then work in a good amount of well-rotted compost. The organic material will make the soil more friable and aerated for better water absorption.

Weeds are undoubtedly an herb's worst enemy. If not controlled from the start, weeds will choke out young plants. A friable soil prior to planting will discourage competition at first. For extra protection, spread two or three inches of mulch around your herbs after they are established. Leaves or straw are good mulching materials, and will prevent weeds from sprouting.

In early fall, work in more compost and manure to ensure a fertile soil for the following year. In cold-climate areas, cover tender perennial herbs for winter protection.

Instead of planting your herbs in helter-skelter fashion, first sketch a simple plan. Even if you're striving for a natural design, a plan will help you in achieving the unstudied look you want.

If you're new to the world of herb gardening, start on a small scale. Experiment with a perennial border, a bare spot between a hedge and lawn, or an unused corner in your vegetable garden. Short of space? Herbs also will grow well in a container on a deck or patio, or on a sunny kitchen windowsill.

During the cold winter months, allow yourself some research time to make a shopping list of wise choices. First, decide whether you want a fragrance garden or a culinary garden, or—if you want to reap the benefits of both—a mix.

Next, select a few herbs to experiment with. Some of the more popular culinary herbs include savory, basil, spearmint, chive, dill, oregano, parsley, tarragon, and sage. Mint, lavender, scented geranium, lemon balm, rosemary, and thyme are delightful choices for a fragrance garden.

Be creative. A lot of goodness can fit into a small space. If used wisely, a 7x12-foot area can accommodate as many as ten different varieties of herbs. Color, texture, and size play important roles in your garden plan, too.

Select a desired color scheme, whether it's a few favorites, or a rainbow mixture. Then cluster those colors that complement each other. Reds, yellows, blues, and purples are great for a splash of bright color. Pale blues and yellows also make a delightful combination. For a softer, more subtle blend of color, try lavender and white.

Give special consideration to the relative size of your plants. To show off the unique beauty of each variety, place taller herbs in the back of the planting area, medium-size plants in the middle, and low-growing herbs up front. Perennials will provide a permanent framework for your garden, with annuals filling in the empty pockets.

Herb Glossary

Since before recorded history, man has boiled, chopped, ground, and dissolved parts of plants looking for the magic cure for everything from irregular heartbeat to insect bites. Blossoms, stems, leaves, and roots were thought to be endowed with mysterious powers. Today, of course, our approach to herbs is considerably more objective. But to the gourmet who fusses over his or her culinary triumphs, herbs are still the magic ingredient that can transform the ordinary into the unforgettable.

For the home gardener, herbs can mean even better-tasting vegetables, as well as delicious aromas and showy leaves and flowers. Keep in mind, though, that almost all herbs need sun and a fairly well-drained soil. Check each herb entry for specific growing instructions.

Basil. Fresh or dried, basil leaves enhance main dishes and salads with spicy taste. Growing to 24 inches tall, this annual provides a bushy fill-in planting for perennial or herb gardens. Start seeds indoors six to eight weeks early, or sow directly outdoors after frost danger has passed. For optimum flavor, harvest the leaves just before the flower buds open.

Chamomile. A fast spreader, this perennial will carpet an area with sprawling foliage. Its perky, daisylike flowers are a good candidate for garden borders and bare spots. Chamomile will grow readily from seed started indoors six to eight weeks early, or directly outside when frost danger has passed. For faster results, plant the root divisions in the early spring.

Borage. The downy foliage and bright, starlike, blue flowers of borage make this annual a must in any garden. Avoid transplanting young plants by sowing seeds directly outside in the spring, where they are to grow. The foliage will grow to 24 inches tall, so prune frequently to keep the plant within bounds. Harvest fresh borage leaves as needed.

Chive. Famous for their many culinary uses, chives are at home in a vegetable or herb garden. Their slender, cylindrical leaves can be snipped daily to enhance any food with a delicate onion flavor. Plant seed or root divisions in the early spring in a sunny area. Once established, divide the chive clumps every few years. Pinch back occasionally for culinary use.

Comfrey. Large bright green leaves and pendulous blue flowers make comfrey an outstanding garden plant. Growing to 30 inches tall, comfrey is best grown in the back of the border or herb garden. This hardy perennial spreads quickly and grows well in both sun and partial shade. Plant seeds or root divisions in the spring. Harvest the plants before they flower.

Dill. This dainty annual will enchant you with its soft, airy branches and feathery foliage. Tiny yellow flowers bloom in early summer, and the plant may grow three feet tall. Sow seeds in shallow furrows in an open area, after all danger of frost has passed. Use fresh leaves in salads or to make dill vinegar. Dried seeds often are used in pickling.

Garlic. A close relative of the onion, the humble garlic plant grows best when it is planted in the late summer or early fall. This way, the plants get a head start in the spring. The following summer, when the tops begin to turn yellow, bend them with the back of a rake. Dig the bulbs when the foliage has turned completely brown.

Coriander. Growing erect to a height of three feet, coriander is another wise choice for the back of a garden border. White flowers and fingerlike foliage will soften the abruptness of a wall or fence line. Seedlings are hard to transplant, so plant seeds directly outside where plants are to remain. When the flower clusters turn brown, it's time to harvest the seeds.

Fennel. The aromatic fennel plant grows about 48 inches high. It's a perennial in warm-climate areas, but in most parts of the country it should be treated as an annual. Plant seeds or transplants outdoors in full sun after all danger of frost has passed. Use fresh leaves as needed for recipes. When the flower heads have turned brown, harvest the seeds.

Lavender. An all-time favorite, lavender is characterized by its sweet aroma. Start seeds indoors ten to 12 weeks early. Germination and survival rates are low, so be sure to sow extra seeds. For faster results, plant divisions. Harvest fresh leaves as needed, and flower heads just before they open. Use lavender with other aromatic herbs to create potpourri and sachets.

Lemon balm. Brush a lemon balm plant with your hands and you'll understand where this perennial gets its name. Each leaf releases a delightful lemon scent. Sow seeds indoors ten to 12 weeks early, or plant directly outdoors in a sunny or partially sunny location. Do not cover the seeds completely when planting, because light is needed for germination.

Oregano. Highlight an oregano plant in the back of a perennial bed. Its oval-shaped leaves are attractive alone, or can set the stage for flowering annuals. Sow seeds directly outdoors in a well-tilled soil after frost danger has passed. Oregano will grow 30 inches tall. Pinch frequently to promote bushier growth. To harvest, clip off leaves as the plants begin to flower.

Marjoram. Plant marjoram along a walkway or a garden edge. When it's stepped on, or clipped with a lawn mower, the foliage will emit a strong perfume. Start seeds eight to ten weeks early, then plant outdoors in a sunny location after frost danger has passed. After the blooms fade, shear back the entire plant several inches to encourage new growth.

Parsley. Plant a clump of parsley near your back door for convenient snipping. Growing to 12 inches tall, the curled foliage of this annual makes a great garden border. Sow seeds directly outside where they are to remain. To speed up germination, soak parsley seeds in warm water for 24 hours before planting. Harvest fresh leaves as needed for salads or garnishes.

Rosemary. The delightfully fragrant rosemary is a tender perennial that should be grown in pots in northern gardens. Because germination is slow, sow seeds indoors in midwinter, or plant nursery-grown roots in early spring. To harvest, cut the plant halfway down the stalk when it is still in bloom. Dry leaves in a well-ventilated area, and store in airtight containers.

Scented geranium. More than 75 kinds of scented geraniums are available, generally divided into six classes: rose, lemon, mint, fruit, spice, and pungent. Start seeds ten to 12 weeks early, or buy transplants. Plant in a sunny location after frost danger has passed. Harvest fresh leaves as needed. To dry, clip leaves in the fall.

Tarragon. A vigorous grower, tarragon can easily grow three feet tall and almost as wide in one season. Sow seeds or plant stem cuttings in a sunny location in early spring. Divide established plants every few years to keep them within bounds and keep your plants mulched to avoid damaging the dense, shallow root system. Use fresh leaves as needed.

Sage. In medieval times, sage was believed to be a cure-all for many diseases. Today, a dose of sage will impart a subtle flavor to soups and main dishes. Sow seeds outdoors in the early spring. Or, buy started plants. In cold-climate areas, a heavy mulch is necessary to protect this semihardy perennial. To harvest, cut back the stem tips when the flowers begin to form.

Tansy. Towering to a height of two to five feet, tansy is best set close to a fence or wall for protection from wind. Seeds are hard to establish, so start from root divisions. Plant in early spring in a sunny location. Because the roots are invasive, they should be confined in a sunken, bottomless container. When the flowers appear, cut and dry them upside down.

Thyme. Use thyme to soften the starkness of a rock garden, or to transform a hard-to-mow area into an easy-care ground cover. Many varieties are available; most species grow only 12 inches tall. Sow seeds indoors four to six weeks early, or plant directly outdoors after frost danger. For speedier results, buy started transplants. Harvest foliage before plants bloom.

Herb Handcrafts

Dried flowers and herbs have a charm and mystique all their own. After the last days of summer have faded, they provide ingredients for aromatic potpourri, dried arrangements, pomander balls, and sachets. Collect and dry herbs and flowers during their growing season. This way, you can preserve and enjoy your fond memories of summer all winter long.

Drying Methods

Air-drying: Cut flowers at midday, when the blooms are at their best. Strip the leaves and gather the flowers in small bunches secured with elastic ties. Hang the bunches upside down in a dark ventilated attic or room for two to three weeks. Avoid picking flowers after a heavy rain or when they're covered with dew.

Some excellent garden choices for this method include cockscomb, larkspur, lavender, annual statice, bells of Ireland, blue sal-

via, Chinese lanterns, globe amaranth, hydrangea, delphinium, yarrow, artemisia, heather, mint, sage, and strawflower.

Air-drying also works well for field flowers such as dock, goldenrod, pampas grass, pearly everlasting, teasel, and tansy.

Silica gel: Great candidates for desiccant drying include zinnias, marigolds, roses, shasta daisies, dahlias, delphiniums, snapdragons, feverfew, and peonies. But remember: The finished product is only as good as the flower specimen you picked.

Place a one- or two-inch base of silica gel granules in the bottom of a coffee can and insert the short cut stem of the flower faceup in the drying medium. Be careful not to overlap any of the petals between flower specimens. Gently sprinkle more of the granules over the flowers until they are completely covered with silica gel to a depth of about one inch. Cover tightly and tape the name of the flower and the date on top of the container. Leave the tin in a dark, dry place until the petals feel brittle and papery; if they don't, replace the cover and let the

flowers dry longer. When they are ready to remove, slowly pour off the silica gel and cup your hand under the flower head. Gently shake off the drying compound and, if necessary, remove stubborn granules with a soft artist's brush. Store the flowers in airtight boxes until ready to use.

For neat storage, insert the erect stem ends in blocks of dry floral foam. To keep dried material in top condition, especially over prolonged periods or when excessive humidity may be a problem, add three to four tablespoons of silica gel to the storage container. If a petal should fall off, dab a small amount of white glue on the end of the petal, then join it to the flower center with tweezers.

Borax: Ordinary household borax may be used as a drying medium. Follow the silica gel directions with two exceptions: Place the flower facedown in the container and leave the lid off while drying. Though less expensive than silica gel, borax takes twice as long to act as a desiccant and doesn't preserve color as well.

Projects

Pomander balls: A pomander or spice ball, *opposite*, is an orange pierced with whole cloves and rolled in a mixture of cinnamon, nutmeg, allspice, and orrisroot (a scent preservative that is available at pharmacies and craft shops). Placed in a clothes closet or trunk, pomanders lend a delightful, spicy fragrance to stored items. When dressed with bright ribbons, they also make wonderful Christmas decorations or gifts.

Potpourri: One of the best ways to use dried flower petals, herbs, and spices is to make your own scented potpourri mixture, *above, left*. The idea is to create your own recipe with a few of your favorite fragrances. To make the potpourri, first collect some fresh rose petals. Clip petals during the summer and dry them in a shady, well-ventilated place. Store the dried petals in airtight containers until you are ready to make the potpourri. Stir the petals every few days.

Next, crush a mixture of herbs such as lavender, orris-root, tonka bean, sandalwood, lemon verbena, and sage until you get a scent combination that pleases you.

Thoroughly mix these ingredients with the dried rose petals and cure in a covered container for five or six weeks, stirring the mixture every few days.

After curing, place the potpourri mix in sachets or store it in jars, boxes, or other covered containers, then place the containers strategically throughout your house. Open the containers whenever you want to fill a room with a pleasant scent. You also can place potpourri in open bowls, but the scent will soon dissipate.

Sachets: Tuck sachets of herbs into bureau drawers or linen closets for sweet-scented results. In these sachets, *above, right*, a dried mixture of lavender, rose geranium, and lemon verbena was used for fill.

Pressed flowers: If you're a real enthusiast of the craft, you'll want to buy a flower press, complete with blotting paper, at a craft shop. Most

people, however, find that a thick telephone book suffices. At one-inch intervals in the book, spread facial tissue on newspaper. Place the flowers flat and avoid overlapping. Cover the flowers with tissue, then newspaper. In this way, the newspaper print will not be picked up by the flowers while they're being pressed.

Repeat the process until the book is filled. If possible, use even thickness of materials on each page for even drying. Remember to include buds and curve some stems and leaves for graceful positioning when dried. Put a weight on the book and store for three to four weeks in a dry, dark place.

Some garden favorites for pressing include daisy, buttercup, verbena, dusty miller, hydrangea, lobelia, delphinium, sweet alyssum, pansy, viola, and fern.

Country Gardens
A Plan for Perennials

Every gardener visualizes his or her lot ablaze with glorious flower color from earliest spring until killing frost, or even year round in mild winter areas. The trouble is, no plant blooms at its best for a full 12 months. However, you can plan and plant combinations of flowers that will take turns providing color. You can use two or three kinds of plants this way even if you have only a tiny corner or strip of earth that doesn't provide enough room for a more conventional border.

Traditionalists use only perennials to achieve their spring-to-fall show of color, but more liberal-minded gardeners mix bulbs, annuals, biennials, herbs, and shrubs such as roses to bolster their perennial plantings.

Draw a rough plot plan, to a scale of ¼ or ½ inch per foot. For every growing season in your area, select an outstanding, easily grown plant to serve as the major or key flower. A good sequence of major flowers might be tulips, iris, peonies, daylilies, phlox, and chrysanthemums. Use these key plants generously in large groupings or drifts. Then pick one or more secondary flowers as fillers. Examples include sweet williams for tulips, daisies for iris, and lythrum for phlox.

Most perennial flowers prefer to grow in a sunny location, but some species thrive in partially shady conditions. In the border **(top)** *Autumn Joy sedum, White Swirls Siberian iris, Goldquelle rudbeckia,* Lobelia splendens, Sanguisorba canadensis, *and astilbe Finale grow in front of the tall Rocket ligularia.*

White Regal lilies, Gold Greenheart heliopsis, and Sir John Falstaff pink phlox create a festival of flowers **(center)** *in late summer. The wildflower* Cimicifuga racemosa *grows in back.*

A spectacular late-summer combination **(bottom)** *includes Golden Showers coreopsis, Miss Lingard phlox, and Cambridge Scarlet bee balm.*

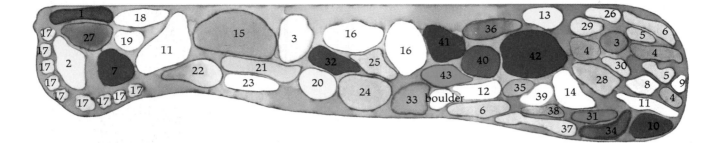

1 Taplow Blue globe thistle, July
2 Feverfew, July-September
3 Goat's Beard (aruncus), June-July
4 Peach Blossom astilbe, June-July
5 Rhineland astilbe, June-August
6 Irrlicht astilbe, June-August
7 Fire astilbe, June-August
8 Ostrich Plume astilbe, June-August
9 White Gloria astilbe, June-August

10 Red Sentinel astilbe, June-August
11 Baby's Tears chrysanthemum, August-September
12 Little Miss Muffet chrysanthemum, July-September
13 Revere chrysanthemum, August-September
14 Cloud 9 chrysanthemum, August-September
15 Sir John Falstaff phlox, July-August
16 Miss Lingard phlox, July-August

17 Silver Mound artemisia, all summer
18 Snakeroot (cimicifuga), July-August
19 Regal lily, June-July
20 Citronella lily, June-July
21 Balloon flower, July-August
22 Senecio adonidifolius, June
23 White bleeding-heart, May-June
24 Pink bleeding-heart, May-June

25 Old-fashioned bleeding-heart, May-June
26 Moonbeam coreopsis, June-August
27 Gold Green-heart heliopsis, July-August
28 Purple globe thistle, July
29 Honeybells hosta, July-August
30 Hosta undulata, July-August
31 Blue Danube stokesia, June-August

32 Chocolate soldier peony, May-June
33 Golden Showers coreopsis, June-August
34 Blue salvia, August
35 Lavender salvia, August
36 Blue veronica, June-September
37 Silver King artemisia, all summer
38 Pink meadowsweet, July-August
39 White baptisia, June

40 Copper Spray helenium, August-September
41 Cambridge Scarlet monarda, July-August
42 Red meadowsweet, July-August
43 Allium sphaerocephalum, May-June

Country Gardens
A Colossus Of Color

For dependable garden color, choose perennials that bloom at the same time and complement each other in height and color. To plan your plant partnerships, study blooming seasons, size at maturity, and flower hues before you plant. Assign tall-growing perennials to spots behind the medium-size plants; save the front of the border for the low growers. To bolster the color, mix in long-blooming annuals and bulbs.

Tall (over 30 inches) background perennials include delphinium, daylilies, hardy lilies, and heliopsis. For mid-border, choose from bee balm, phlox, veronica, baby's-breath, and rudbeckia. And for the edging, try cushion chrysanthemums, dwarf iris, astilbe, pinks, or Silver Mound artemisia.

Plant in drifts or clumps, not in rows. Use at least three identical specimens in each clump of low-growing flowers—one plant of a small-size variety will not give you much flower impact. Large perennials like peony, loosestrife, gas plant, and baptisia can be planted singly.

Showy blue balloon flowers (top) brighten the garden during July and August. Balloon flowers grow about 20 inches tall and require a sunny location for best growth.

The sunny yellow flowers of evening primrose (center) appear from June till August. Hardy primrose plants prefer a sunny location with well-drained, slightly sandy soil. The evening primrose grows to about 18 inches tall.

The regal hardy lily (bottom) adds a touch of elegance along a garden path during June and July. Lilies require very little care and are available in a host of colors and bicolors.

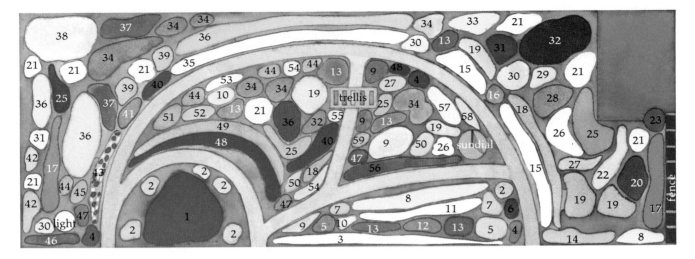

1 Annual salvia,
summer
2 Artemisia, June-
September
3 White petunia,
summer
4 Sedum, July-
August
5 Balloon flower,
July-August
6 Gaillardia, June-
August

7 Marigold,
summer
8 Evening primrose,
June-August
9 Sweet william,
June-July
10 Feverfew, June-
August
11 Snapdragon,
summer
12 Siberian iris,
June

13 Mum,
September
14 Forget-me-not,
May-July
15 Alyssum,
summer
16 Columbine,
June-July
17 Baptisia, June
18 Pink petunia,
summer
19 Phlox, July

September
20 Bee balm, July-
August
21 White dahlia,
July-September
22 Loosestrife,
June-July
23 Hibiscus, July-
August
24 Strawberry bed
25 Delphinium,
June

26 Shasta daisy,
June-August
27 Blue salvia,
July-September
28 Bleeding-heart,
May-June
29 Honeysuckle
shrub
30 Bearded iris,
May-June
31 Chinese lantern,
July-August
32 Maltese cross,
May-July
33 Nerine lily,
August
34 Peony, May-
June
35 Astilbe, June-
July
36 Daylily, June-
September
37 Cosmos, summer
38 Hollyhock, July-
September
39 Lupine, June-
August
40 Zinnia, summer
41 Heliotrope,
June-September
42 Sweet pea,
May-June

43 Jacob's-coat,
May-September
44 Coralbells,
May-June
45 Nicotiana,
summer
46 Nierembergia,
summer
47 Geranium,
May-June
48 Lobelia,
August-September
49 Dusty miller,
June-September
50 Yarrow, June-
September
51 Pinks, June-
September
52 Strawflower,
July-September
53 Edelweiss, June-
July
54 Virginia
bluebell, May-June
55 Chive, May-
June
56 Nasturtium,
summer
57 Hardy lily,
June-September
58 Ageratum,
June-September
59 Tarragon, June

Country Gardens
Vegetables: Growing Basics

A well-cared-for vegetable garden can be as visually attractive as it is productive. In fact, many vegetable gardens are just as eye-catching as well-organized flower beds. To keep your vegetable plot in top form, remember these basic pointers.

First, soil condition is the most critical element in the success of a vegetable garden. The quality and quantity of the crop is directly dependent on what the soil offers in terms of a good root environment and nutrition. The plant's roots must be able to grow easily.

If you have an existing vegetable garden, your soil is probably in good shape, but if you are breaking new ground, you may find soil that's less than ideal the first year. If the ground needs improvement, turn the soil a full-spade depth, or till as deeply as possible. Add a liberal amount of organic material and turn it under. Leaves, grass clippings, well-rotted manure, compost, straw, and leafy kitchen scraps are all good soil amendments.

Ideally, garden soil should be turned in the late fall. This takes the heavy load off the next spring's gardening effort. Also, the soil will be in much better condition for planting.

Don't be stingy with water early in the season. At this time, roots are shallow, and if allowed to dry, the plants will go into a hard-to-break early dormancy. Later on, when roots are deep, watering is important, but not critical.

If drought is a problem in your area, you may want to install a drip irrigation system. These systems are designed to deliver water in small quantities under low pressure to where it does the most good—the roots.

Some vegetables do best with cool-weather starts; others prefer warm weather. Before you plant, find out the average dates of the last frost in spring and the first in the fall for your area. You can plant cool-weather crops one month before the last predicted spring frost. These include beets, broccoli, cabbage, carrots, lettuce, onions, peas, potatoes, spinach, and radishes.

Warm-weather crops should not be planted until all frost danger has passed. Beans, corn, cucumbers, peppers, tomatoes, and squash are included in the warm-weather category.

Country Gardens
Vegetables: Multi-Harvest Ideas

Truly successful gardeners plan their vegetable gardens so they get two or three major harvests in one season. When one crop matures, another is planted immediately. And, whenever possible, two crops with different maturity dates are planted together for a staggered harvest. To ensure continuous production, garden space is never allowed to go empty.

This garden, *right* and *above,* is a perfect example of multiple-harvest planning. The larger of the two beds measures 10x16 feet and is planted with cool-season crops in early April. The crops include spinach, lettuce, beets, radishes, carrots, onions, and peas. By late May, most of these crops are harvested and

warm-weather crops are planted. They include cucumbers, beans, cantaloupes, and another crop of carrots. Cool-season crops that have not been harvested by late May have warm-weather crops planted around them. For example, in mid-May most of the pea vines are still producing abundantly. Thus, tomato transplants are tucked in between the rows of peas. As soon as the pea vines and supports are removed, the tomatoes are allowed to fill in.

The smaller bed, which measures 5x8 feet, is planted with crops that take a long time to mature. Here, vegetables such as eggplant, broccoli, cabbage, and corn grow undisturbed until harvesttime.

Vegetables: A Two-Year Plan

I f you have the land and don't mind a little extra work, why not expand your garden space and bring in a bumper crop of homegrown vegetables.

Thinking big has many advantages. To begin with, you have enough room to grow the highly rewarding perennial crops such as asparagus and rhubarb. Even better, you can devote part of the garden area to growing small fruit. Eating homegrown strawberries, raspberries, or grapes is a pleasure your family will long remember. A larger garden also means you can extend your harvest by growing plenty of vegetables to store for wintertime use.

Potatoes, pumpkins, and many winter squashes are too space-demanding for small gardens but are excellent storage crops.

Although this garden measures a whopping 55x80 feet, it still employs a lot of important space-saving techniques. Quick-growing cool-season crops like lettuce, onions, and beets are all interplanted with the slower-growing broccoli and cabbage plants, *right*. As the broccoli and cabbages mature, the cool-weather crops are harvested from the area.

Vegetables such as peas, beans, spinach, lettuce, onions, carrots, and parsnips are grown in wide rows to increase yields.

307

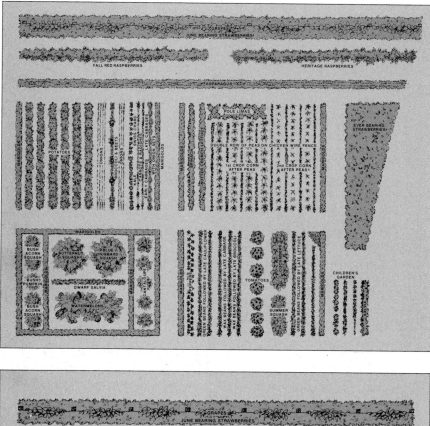

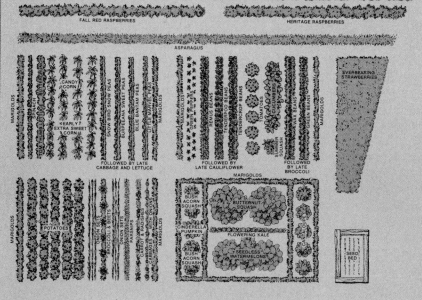

With a garden as large as this one, it's important to keep the gardening chores to a minimum. The bulk of the land was mulched with several inches of spoiled hay to keep in soil moisture and smother weeds. Black plastic mulch was used under the melons and tomatoes.

To make watering more efficient and less time consuming, a drip irrigation system was installed under the mulch in three of the four main garden areas. The fourth garden section, which contained the vine crops, was then the only section that needed any hand watering.

Perhaps the key to this garden's great success lies in the fact that it was planned completely before planting. The garden plans, *left*, show how the garden was designed to allow for yearly crop rotation. They also show how vegetable garden space can be creatively shuffled to add or delete a particular crop. For instance, after the first-season garden, *top*, was finished, the family discovered that they didn't eat the Swiss chard or kale. So, before planting the second year's garden, the family removed these crops from the plan and added a wide row of parsnips, *bottom*.

Credits

Designers, Architects, and Photographers

The following is a list by page number of the interior designers, project designers, architects, and photographers whose work appears in this book. We extend our thanks and appreciation to all of these individuals for their creative talents and expertise.
Note: Photographers' names appear in italics.

Pages 6-7
Ross Chapple
Pages 8-9
Maris/Semel
Pages 10-11
Hopkins Associates
Pages 14-25
Marjorie C. Penny Interiors
Maris/Semel
Pages 26-33
Patricia Payne, ASID
Maris/Semel
Pages 34-41
Claudia Sargent
Maris/Semel
Pages 42-49
Mary Ann Kovac
Jessie Walker
Pages 50-55
Marjorie C. Penny Interiors
Maris/Semel
Pages 56-59
Jessie Walker
Pages 60-63
Hopkins Associates
Page 67
Jim Hedrich
Pages 68-73
Thomas Hooper

Pages 74-75
Bradley Olman
Pages 76-83
Jessie Walker
Pages 88-93
Hopkins Associates
Exterior locations:
Living History Farms,
Des Moines, Iowa
Pages 94-95
Robert E. Dittmer
Mike Dieter, Inc.
Pages 96-97
George Ceolla
Pages 98-99
Hopkins Associates
Pages 100-103
Robert E. Dittmer
Mike Dieter, Inc.
Pages 104-105
George Ceolla
Pages 106-107
Robert E. Dittmer
Mike Dieter, Inc.
Pages 110-125
Jessie Walker
Pages 126-127
Quilt courtesy of
Judy Murphy
Perry Struse
Pages 128-135
Jessie Walker
Pages 138-139
John Medicus
Maris/Semel
Page 140
Patricia Payne, ASID
Maris/Semel
Page 141
Joyce Niewoehner
Jessie Walker

Page 142
Mary Anne Thomson
Jessie Walker
Page 143
Mary Ann Kovac
Jessie Walker
Page 144
(Top) Raymond Waites
Thomas Hooper
(Bottom) Jim and Pat Knocke
Hopkins Associates
Page 145
Linda and Carter Knipping
Jessie Walker
Page 146
(Top) Joyce Niewoehner
Jessie Walker
(Bottom) Mary Anne Thomson
Hopkins Associates
Page 147
Mary Anne Thomson
Jessie Walker
Page 148
Suzanne Worsham,
Patience Corner
Ross Chapple
Page 149
(Top) Bierly-Drake Associates
Maris/Semel
(Bottom) Mary Anne Thomson
Jessie Walker
Page 150
Patricia Payne, ASID
Maris/Semel
Page 151
(Top) Boston Jr. League
Showhouse; Linda A. Levy/
Interiors of Wellesley
(Bottom) Marjorie C. Penny
Interiors
Maris/Semel
Pages 152-153
Stencil: Jim Boleach/Stencil
Magic. Projects: Phyllis
Dunstan. *Hedrich-Blessing*

Credits
(continued)

Pages 214-215
Bernice Lasovick
Maris/Semel
Page 216
Suzanne Worsham
Ross Chapple
Page 217
Jeffrey Charnak
Maris/Semel
Pages 218-219
Ristomatti Ratia
Bradley Olman
Pages 220-221
Tedrick and Bennett
Gordon
Pages 226-229
Bill Helms
Pages 230-235
Architect: Architectural
Period Houses, Inc.
Builder: Howard Atkinson
Maris/Semel
Pages 236-239
Architect: David Howard
Ross Chapple
Pages 240-243
Architect: Russell Scott
Burditt
Harry Hartman
Pages 244-251
Suzanne Moore-Wollum
Hopkins Associates
Pages 252-255
Jacques Campbell
Contractor:
Charles T. Skillern
E. Alan McGee
Pages 256-267
Illustrations: Greg Hargreaves

Pages 274-275
Garden design: Sybil Ittman
Maris/Semel
Pages 276-277
Garden design:
Nancy Ann Whiting
Chuck Ashley
Pages 278-281
Garden design:
Alice and Cliff Grant
Ross Chapple
Page 282
Photographed at Martin/
Viette Nursery and Brooklyn
Botanic Garden
Maris/Semel
Page 283
Produced in cooperation with
the Netherlands Flower-Bulb
Institute
Hopkins Associates
Pages 286-287
Hopkins Associates
Pages 288-289
Garden design: Margy Mirick
Maris/Semel
Pages 290-291
Garden design:
Virginia Colby
Bill Helms
Pages 292-297
Maris/Semel
Pages 298-299
Garden design:
Fred McGourty
Maris/Semel
Pages 300-301
Garden design:
Ronnie Winsor
Hopkins Associates

Pages 302-303
Garden design: John Davies
Bill Helms
Pages 304-305
Garden design: Don Peschke
Peter Krumhardt
Pages 306-309
Garden design: Jon Snyder
Hopkins Associates

Field Editors

Our thanks to the following
Better Homes and Gardens® Field
Editors for their valuable assis-
tance in locating homes,
gardens, crafts, and collectibles
for photography.

Estelle Bond Guralnick
Mary Anne Thomson
Patricia Carpenter
Barbara Cathcart
Eileen Deymier
Helen Heitkamp
Bonnie Maharam
Ruth Reiter
Jessie Walker Associates

Index

Page numbers in italics refer to photographs or to illustrated text.